The Art of Financial Terrain

Mastering Sector and Industry Analysis

Nathan Venture, D

Contents

Introduction

Sector and industry analysis begins with a simple recognition: a company does not operate in a vacuum. Its revenues are shaped by the demand profile of its end market, its margins are constrained or expanded by competitive structure, and its valuation is influenced by the way investors compare it with other businesses facing similar conditions. A strong management team can improve execution, but it cannot fully escape the economics of the field in which it competes.

That is why a stock's story is never only about the stock itself. A retailer can report healthy same-store sales and still struggle if consumer spending weakens across the industry. A bank can post higher earnings and still face pressure if credit costs rise throughout the sector. A manufacturer may appear inexpensive on earnings alone, yet deserve a lower multiple because the industry is capital intensive, cyclical, or exposed to pricing competition. The surrounding terrain matters because it helps determine whether a company's results are durable, repeatable, and properly valued.

For investors, this context improves judgment in three ways. First, it sharpens earnings interpretation. When a company beats expectations, the key question is whether the result reflects a genuine competitive advantage or merely a favorable industry backdrop. Second, it improves forecasting. Industry conditions often change more slowly than quarterly headlines, which makes them useful for framing realistic expectations. Third, it reduces false comparisons. Two companies can both be profitable and growing, yet belong to industries with very different economics, risk profiles, and valuation ranges.

Sector analysis also helps separate what is company-specific from what is systemic. If margins compress across an entire industry, the cause is often not a single flawed business model but a broader change in input costs, demand, regulation, or pricing power. If one company consistently outperforms its peers, the analyst can ask whether the gap comes from scale, product mix, customer retention, capital discipline, or simply temporary timing. In this way, sector and industry study act as a filter that converts raw financial data into a more useful interpretation of business quality.

The importance of this filter increases when markets become more selective. During broad rallies, weak businesses can rise with strong ones. During downturns, high-quality companies may be sold alongside lower-quality peers. In both cases, investors who ignore industry context risk confusing price movement with fundamental strength. A sector-aware approach does not eliminate uncertainty, but it improves the odds of distinguishing resilient businesses from those merely carried by favorable conditions.

There is also a practical reason professionals rely on this framework: it makes research more efficient. Instead of examining every company as if it were unique, analysts can begin with the economic logic of the sector, then narrow the field to the industries and subindustries most likely to reward closer study. That sequence saves time, improves comparability, and helps prevent the common error of applying a one-size-fits-all valuation standard to businesses with very different operating realities.

In agriculture and resource policy, researchers have long relied on sectoral disaggregation because aggregated data can hide the effects of policy and market changes on specific activities [4]. The same principle applies in financial analysis. Broad averages can obscure the forces that matter most to a company's earnings power. A sector lens does not replace company analysis; it gives company analysis a frame of reference.

That frame of reference becomes especially valuable when markets are noisy. Short-term narratives often focus on headlines, but the deeper question is whether the underlying industry structure supports or undermines long-term value creation. Investors who learn to read that structure gain a more stable basis for deciding what deserves attention, what deserves caution, and what deserves a deeper valuation review.

Chapter 1: Why Sector and Industry Analysis Matters

Before a company's numbers can be interpreted correctly, they have to be placed in the setting that gives them meaning. Revenue momentum, margin behavior, capital needs, and even management guidance are all shaped by the business environment surrounding the firm, not just by decisions made inside it. That is why sector and industry analysis is not an optional overlay but a necessary frame of reference for reading financial statements and market expectations. It helps separate what is idiosyncratic from what is structural, what is temporary from what is persistent, and what is genuinely improving from what is merely being lifted by favorable conditions.

The limits of standalone company analysis

Standalone company analysis can be useful, but it is often incomplete because a business's reported results are filtered through conditions it does not fully control. A retailer may post slower same-store sales not because its brand has suddenly weakened, but because the entire category is being pressured by weak consumer spending, changing shopping habits, or excess promotional activity. A bank may appear to be managing credit well until rising rates, funding costs, or a loosening of lending standards reveal that the surrounding environment has changed. In both cases, the company's operating record is real, yet the interpretation of that record is distorted if it is separated from the sector and industry setting that produced it.

One of the biggest limits of looking only at the company is that many financial metrics are relative, not absolute. Revenue growth, margin expansion, and earnings surprises can look impressive in isolation while still being ordinary or even weak compared with peers. A firm that grows earnings 8% in a year may seem healthy, but if comparable companies in the same industry are growing 15% because of stronger demand or better pricing, that company is actually losing ground. The reverse is also true: a business can report flat results in a difficult industry and still be outperforming competitors. Without an industry frame of reference, investors risk confusing resilience with mediocrity, or temporary tailwinds with durable strength.

Company-specific analysis also tends to understate how much business models are shaped by industry economics. Capital intensity, regulatory burden, customer concentration, pricing power, and exposure to commodity inputs all influence what a company can earn and how stable those earnings will be. Two firms can have similar revenue growth but very different earnings quality if one operates in a high-fixed-cost environment and the other in a lighter, more flexible model. A software company and a utility may both be profitable, yet they deserve different expectations because their competitive structures, reinvestment needs, and risk profiles are not comparable. Sector and industry analysis helps identify which results are likely to persist and which are simply a reflection of favorable conditions that may not last.

This matters especially when investors try to judge valuation. A stock rarely trades on its numbers alone; it trades on how those numbers compare with what the market expects from similar businesses. If an industry is in a period of strong demand, investors may assign higher multiples to firms that are merely keeping pace with the group. If an industry is under pressure, even a high-quality company may trade at a discount because future earnings are assumed to be harder to sustain. Descriptive work on market valuation and risk indicators has shown how much interpretation depends on the surrounding market context rather than on a single firm's financial statements [11]. That is why a low price-to-earnings ratio can signal opportunity in one setting and structural weakness in another.

Another weakness of standalone analysis is that it can over-credit management for outcomes driven largely by the environment. Good executives matter, but they do not set input prices, consumer demand, interest rates, or industry-wide capacity. When margins expand across an entire sector, the improvement may reflect a favorable cost cycle, pricing discipline, or a temporary supply shortage rather than a unique operational advantage. When margins contract across the group, even strong operators can look worse before they have actually lost competitive position. Investors who focus only on the company can mistake cyclical effects for strategic skill, or mistake temporary pressure for a permanent deterioration in execution.

The problem becomes more serious when analysts use historical company data without asking whether the underlying industry regime has changed. A business that once earned stable returns may face a very different future if technology, regulation, customer behavior, or capital requirements have shifted. In agriculture, for example, researchers emphasize that production systems must be assessed as combinations of philosophy, risk, and adaptability rather than as isolated outputs, because environmental and operational conditions alter the economics of the entire system [9]. The same logic applies in equity analysis: a company's past performance is informative, but it is not self-explanatory. The analyst still has to ask whether the company's reported results are being amplified or constrained by the terrain around it.

For this reason, standalone company analysis should be treated as the starting point, not the full method. It identifies what a business reported; sector and industry analysis helps explain why those results occurred and whether they are likely to repeat. That distinction improves forecasting, sharpens valuation judgments, and reduces the odds of building an investment case on numbers that are accurate but misleading. The company matters, but the company is never the whole market environment in which those numbers were created.

How sectors and industries influence earnings quality and valuation

Earnings quality is never judged in a vacuum. Two companies can report the same growth rate and the same margin expansion while presenting very different levels of underlying durability. In one industry, revenue may be recurring, pricing may be disciplined, and customer relationships may be sticky enough that reported earnings closely track economic reality. In another, the same pattern may be supported by aggressive discounting, channel stuffing, loose credit terms, or temporary demand pull-forward. Sector and industry context helps determine whether earnings are being generated by repeatable operating strength or by conditions that are unlikely to persist. That distinction matters because valuation is built on expectations about future cash flows, not merely on the latest accounting result.

The structure of an industry shapes how much earnings can be trusted. Businesses with high switching costs, subscription models, or long-term contracts often produce earnings that are more stable and easier to forecast because customers are less likely to leave and revenue visibility is higher. By contrast, industries with low switching costs and intense price competition tend to experience more volatile margins and more management pressure to smooth results. In retail banking, for example, customer retention is closely tied to revenue stability and cost efficiency, which is why switching behavior is not just a marketing issue but a driver of earnings persistence [2]. When customer loyalty is fragile, earnings can deteriorate quickly even if headline revenue appears healthy for a time.

Industry economics also influence how much discretion management has over reported earnings. In some sectors, accounting choices and operating judgments can significantly affect the appearance of performance. This does not mean the numbers are unreliable by default, but it does mean investors must ask whether earnings reflect underlying demand or the timing of recognition, reserve building, capitalization, and expense classification. Research on financial reporting shows that reporting quality is shaped by the institutional and regulatory environment, and that incentives and disclosure conditions affect the complexity and comparability of reported results [16][17]. For investors, the practical implication is straightforward: the same net income figure can mean very different things depending on the sector's reporting conventions and the competitive pressure managers face.

Valuation multiples are similarly conditioned by sector and industry characteristics. A company is not assigned a price-to-earnings ratio solely because of its growth rate; the market is also pricing the durability of that growth, the sensitivity of margins, the need for reinvestment, and the risk that current earnings will revert. Capital-light businesses with recurring revenue and modest working capital needs often deserve higher multiples because a larger share of reported earnings can become free cash flow. Capital-intensive industries, by contrast, may show respectable accounting profits while consuming substantial cash to sustain operations, leaving less economic value for shareholders. In those cases, a low multiple may reflect not pessimism but realism about reinvestment requirements and the cyclicality of returns.

Industry context also affects the interpretation of margin quality. A rising operating margin is not automatically a sign of superior execution if the entire sector is benefiting from temporary input-cost relief, easy comparisons, or an unusually favorable demand backdrop. Likewise, a margin decline may not signal deterioration in competitive position if the industry is absorbing a short-term shock that affects all participants. The key question is whether the margin change comes from structural advantage or from the phase of the cycle. Industries with durable pricing power can often pass through inflation and preserve margins, while industries with commoditized products may see reported profitability fluctuate sharply as costs and prices move out of sync.

Accounting quality and valuation quality are linked because investors pay for earnings that can be converted into cash and sustained over time. In sectors where revenue is lumpy, customer churn is high, or inventories can be built ahead of demand, reported earnings may overstate economic strength for extended periods. In sectors with recurring billing, regulated returns, or strong contract visibility, earnings may be a better proxy for future cash generation. This is why analysts often give more weight to cash flow, reserve adequacy, deferred revenue trends, or backlog quality in certain industries than they would in others. The point is not that one sector is inherently better than another, but that each sector creates its own pattern of earnings reliability and valuation logic.

Investors who ignore these differences often compare companies using a single yardstick that does not fit the business model. They may penalize a stable, mature company for slower growth even when its earnings are highly dependable, or they may reward a fast-growing company with a rich multiple even though its earnings are fragile and highly dependent on favorable conditions. Sector and industry analysis reduces those errors by showing which earnings are likely to persist, which are likely to mean-revert, and which are supported by structural advantages. That is the foundation for interpreting both earnings quality and valuation with greater precision.

Why different market participants use sector analysis differently

Different market participants use sector analysis differently because they are solving different problems. A long-term value investor is usually trying to estimate durable cash generation and a margin of safety, so the sector lens helps identify whether a business operates in an environment that supports stable returns on capital or compresses them over time. A trader, by contrast, may care less about long-run franchise quality and more about whether money is rotating into or out of a group over the next few weeks or months. A retirement planner may focus on income reliability, inflation sensitivity, and drawdown risk, while a financial advisor may use sector exposure to keep client portfolios diversified and aligned with risk tolerance. The analysis framework is similar, but the decision horizon changes the questions that matter most.

For fundamental analysts, sector work is often about separating company-specific performance from industry-wide conditions. That distinction matters because a strong earnings report can mean very different things depending on the setting. In a favorable sector, even average operators can look healthy as pricing, demand, and investor sentiment all rise together. In a difficult sector, an apparently weak result may still represent outperformance if peers are suffering from the same cost pressures or demand slowdown. This is why sector analysis is not just a background check on the business; it is a way to judge whether the company is winning or merely drifting with the tide.

Institutional investors use sector analysis in a more systematic way than many individuals. Portfolio managers compare industries to decide where capital should be overweighted, underweighted, or avoided entirely. They also use sector context to interpret earnings revisions, estimate how much of a company's growth is cyclical versus structural, and decide whether a valuation premium is justified. In practice, that means a manager may be willing to pay more for a business in a sector with recurring demand, high switching costs, and disciplined competition than for a similarly growing company in a sector where margins tend to be unstable. Sector analysis becomes a tool for ranking opportunity, not just for labeling businesses.

Traders use the same information with a different time frame and a different emphasis. They often look for leadership, relative strength, and momentum within a sector because those signals can reveal where capital is flowing before the broader market fully recognizes it. A trader may not need to know every detail of a company's long-term competitive position if the sector is already being repriced around interest rates, commodity prices, policy changes, or earnings surprises. What matters is whether the group is attracting attention and whether that attention is likely to persist long enough to create a tradable move. In that setting, sector analysis helps identify the most responsive names and avoid stocks trapped in weak groups.

Credit investors and lenders use sector analysis to judge downside risk. Their focus is not only on earnings growth but also on the consistency of cash flow, the resilience of demand, and the likelihood that a downturn will impair debt service. A business in a volatile sector may still be investable if leverage is modest and liquidity is strong, but a similar balance sheet in a more cyclical or capital-intensive industry can become fragile quickly. Sector context therefore shapes covenant expectations, default assumptions, and the amount of stress that a lender should build into the analysis.

Regulatory and accounting considerations also affect how different participants interpret sector data. Some industries are more exposed to policy changes, disclosure requirements, or shifts in enforcement than others, so reported results can be influenced by the rules governing the business as much as by operating performance. Ray Ball's discussion of accounting scandals shows that the same corporate behavior can look different when viewed through market incentives versus regulatory oversight [19]. That matters for sector analysis because some industries are more prone to aggressive accounting, more dependent on estimates, or more sensitive to changes in reporting standards. A cautious analyst does not treat reported numbers as equally informative across all sectors.

The practical implication is that sector analysis is not a single discipline with one correct use. It is a flexible framework that adapts to the analyst's objective. The value investor uses it to test durability and valuation discipline. The trader uses it to locate momentum and timing opportunities. The advisor uses it to manage portfolio balance and client-specific risk. The earnings-focused analyst uses it to judge whether a surprise is truly meaningful or simply normal for the industry. Even when the same data set is being reviewed, the interpretation changes because the decision being made changes. That is why sector analysis becomes more useful, not less, as the sophistication of the market participant increases.

Common mistakes investors make when ignoring industry context

One of the most common mistakes investors make is treating a company's financial results as if they were produced in isolation, when in reality they are often the product of a broader industry setting. A business can look unusually strong simply because it sits in a favorable part of the cycle, benefits from temporary supply shortages, or operates in a market where competitors are restraining capacity. The reverse is also true: a fundamentally sound company can appear disappointing when the entire industry is facing margin pressure, weak demand, or a period of heavy reinvestment. When investors ignore that context, they risk confusing a cyclical tailwind for durable competitive advantage, or a temporary setback for permanent deterioration.

This error shows up most clearly in valuation work. A low multiple may look attractive on the surface, but if the industry is structurally challenged, that multiple may be justified by declining economics rather than mispricing. Likewise, a high multiple may seem excessive until it is compared with an industry that consistently produces above-average returns on capital, recurring revenue, and stronger visibility into future cash flows. The mistake is not merely paying too much or too little; it is using the wrong frame of reference. Valuation is always relative to growth, risk, and quality, and those traits are heavily shaped by industry conditions.

Ignoring industry context also leads investors to misread earnings quality. In some sectors, reported earnings are closely tied to real economic performance because pricing is stable, customer demand is predictable, and working capital requirements are manageable. In others, earnings can be distorted by channel incentives, aggressive discounting, inventory swings, or accounting choices that temporarily smooth volatility. Research on financial reporting quality has shown that reporting outcomes are intertwined with broader institutional and country attributes rather than being explained by accounting rules alone [16]. That same principle applies at the industry level: the environment surrounding a business influences how reliable its reported numbers are and how much confidence investors should place in them.

Another mistake is assuming that all growth is equally valuable. Investors often celebrate revenue expansion without asking whether the industry is absorbing that growth through lower margins, heavier capital spending, or rising customer acquisition costs. In a mature or over-crowded industry, growth can be expensive and fragile. In a concentrated industry with barriers to entry, growth may be more profitable and more durable. Without that distinction, investors may overpay for companies that are growing quickly but not efficiently, while overlooking slower-growing firms that generate superior returns because their industry structure supports better economics.

Industry context matters just as much when judging risk. A company with moderate leverage may look safe until investors recognize that it belongs to a sector exposed to commodity swings, regulatory changes, funding stress, or rapid technological disruption. In financial services, for example, assessing soundness requires attention to the broader sector environment, because balance-sheet strength, liquidity, and profitability can shift quickly when conditions change [23][24]. The same company could be viewed very differently depending on whether the industry is stable, highly cyclical, or vulnerable to shocks. Investors who ignore this often underestimate downside risk because they analyze the balance sheet without analyzing the business model that supports it.

There is also a behavioral trap in comparing companies from different industries as though their metrics mean the same thing everywhere. A margin level, payout ratio, or growth rate that looks mediocre in one field may be outstanding in another. A capital-intensive business may deserve a lower return profile than a software-like model with low reinvestment needs, but that does not make it inferior if it produces reliable cash and serves a necessary market. Cross-industry comparisons can be useful only when the investor adjusts for business structure, not when the numbers are read literally and ranked mechanically. Many poor decisions begin with a spreadsheet that is technically correct but economically naive.

Finally, investors often mistake industry noise for company-specific insight. An earnings miss may reflect temporary pricing pressure across the whole group rather than a unique failure in execution. A guidance cut may simply acknowledge a weaker demand backdrop that every peer is facing. When investors fail to separate company actions from industry conditions, they may reward or punish management for forces it does not control. That leads to distorted conclusions about leadership quality, competitive position, and future prospects. The better habit is to ask, before forming a judgment, whether the company's result is unusual for the industry or merely typical of the environment it is operating in.

Chapter 2: The Market Map—How Sectors, Industries, and Subindustries Fit Together

Before a company can be compared intelligently, it has to be placed on the right part of the map. The labels investors use for sectors, industries, and subindustries are more than administrative categories; they are the organizing framework that determines which businesses are truly comparable, which trends are shared, and which risks are being priced across a group rather than inside a single name. That structure matters because financial analysis is often a comparative exercise: margins, growth rates, capital intensity, and valuation multiples only become meaningful when they are viewed against a relevant peer set.

Sector, industry, and subindustry definitions

At the broadest level, a sector is a large grouping of businesses that share similar economic drivers, while an industry is a narrower grouping inside that sector made up of firms that compete in closely related lines of business. A subindustry is narrower still, capturing companies with even more specific product sets, customer bases, or operating models. These labels matter because they define the pool of peers against which a company's performance, valuation, and risk profile are judged. A software company serving hospitals does not belong in the same analytical bucket as a software company serving consumers, even if both are officially classified as technology firms. The classification tells you where to look first; it does not tell you everything, but it prevents you from starting in the wrong place.

The distinction becomes more useful when you think about what actually moves earnings. Sector-level forces tend to be broad and macro-sensitive: interest rates, commodity prices, regulation, consumer spending, or credit conditions. Industry-level forces are more specific: pricing power, capacity utilization, customer concentration, product substitution, and the pace of innovation. Subindustry forces are narrower still and often determine the details that matter most for forecasting, such as reimbursement rules for a medical device niche, freight rates for a shipping segment, or ad spending trends for a particular digital platform category. The deeper you go, the more precise the comparison becomes, and the less likely you are to mistake a group-wide trend for a company-specific advantage.

In practice, investors use these labels to build a hierarchy of analysis. The sector gives the first directional context: is the broader environment favorable or unfavorable? The industry refines that view: are businesses with similar economics seeing the same pressure or tailwind? The subindustry then helps separate winners from laggards inside a crowded field. This is especially important when reported results look strong or weak for reasons that are invisible without peer context. A company may appear to be gaining share when it is really benefiting from a subindustry-wide demand surge. Another may appear to be underperforming when its group is facing a temporary margin squeeze that affects everyone in the category.

Classification systems are also practical tools for screening and benchmarking. They allow investors to compare revenue growth, operating margins, capital intensity, leverage, and valuation multiples across businesses that face roughly similar conditions. Without that structure, comparisons can become misleading very quickly. A capital-light service business and a capital-intensive manufacturer may both trade at 20 times earnings, but that multiple may reflect very different expectations for reinvestment needs, cyclicality, and resilience. The label attached to the company does not create comparability by itself, but it helps define a reasonable comparison set and keeps the analysis grounded in economics rather than in superficial similarity.

This is why classification systems are useful even though they are imperfect. Real businesses often span more than one category, and many large companies have multiple operating segments that touch different markets. A single firm may sell both hardware and software, serve both consumers and enterprises, or operate in both domestic and international markets. In those cases, the formal label is only a starting point. The analyst still has to determine which revenue stream matters most, which segment drives margins, and which part of the business is most exposed to the cycle. The point is not to force every company into a neat box; it is to use the box as a disciplined way to begin asking better questions.

That discipline matters because market participants often overstate the meaning of the label while underestimating the meaning of the underlying business model. A company can sit in the same broad sector as its peers and still behave very differently because of brand strength, customer retention, pricing structure, or geographic mix. Research on brand systems emphasizes that a brand is not just a name or image, but a managed system of signals and relationships that shapes how value is created and protected over time [26]. In sector and industry analysis, that idea translates into a simple point: the formal category tells you where the company belongs, but the business model tells you how it competes inside that category.

For that reason, the most useful definition is not merely administrative. A sector is a broad economic environment, an industry is a competitive arena within that environment, and a subindustry is a more precise competitive subset where the drivers of performance are even more similar. Those distinctions help investors separate structural forces from company-specific execution, choose the right peer group, and avoid comparing businesses whose financial statements may look alike while their economics differ in important ways.

How classification systems are used in practice

Classification systems are used in practice to turn a large, messy equity universe into a workable research map. In most professional settings, the first step is not asking whether a company is "good" or "bad," but where it belongs in the classification hierarchy and whether that placement is consistent with the economic drivers that matter most. A company's label determines its peer set, its benchmark, the analyst coverage it receives, and the comparisons used to judge growth, margins, leverage, and valuation. That makes classification a functional tool, not just a naming convention.

In day-to-day analysis, classification systems help investors avoid comparing businesses that may look similar on the surface but behave very differently underneath. A payments processor, a regional bank, and a consumer finance platform all touch financial services, yet their earnings drivers, capital needs, and sensitivity to credit conditions are not interchangeable. Likewise, two firms inside a broad technology bucket may share innovation themes but differ sharply in recurring revenue, customer concentration, and cyclicality. The practical value of classification is that it narrows the field to companies whose financial statements are likely to respond to the same forces, making relative analysis more meaningful.

Most market participants rely on some version of a standardized taxonomy so that research, portfolio construction, and performance attribution can be communicated consistently across firms and systems. The exact labels vary by provider, but the purpose is similar: create a common language for sorting companies by primary business activity. This matters because a portfolio manager cannot assess sector exposure without a stable map of what belongs where, and an analyst cannot compare valuation multiples intelligently without knowing whether the companies being compared are truly exposed to the same demand drivers, cost structures, and regulatory regimes. Classification also supports screening, since investors often begin with a sector or industry filter before moving to deeper fundamental work.

In practice, however, the classification assigned to a company is not always a perfect reflection of how the business actually behaves. Many firms operate across multiple lines of business, and the classification usually follows the segment that contributes the largest share of revenue, earnings, or market perception, even if another segment is more important to future growth. That can create friction between the label and the economics. A company may be categorized one way for administrative consistency while the market prices it according to a different narrative, especially when a newer business line begins to dominate investor attention. This is why serious analysts treat classification as a starting point rather than a final answer.

Reclassification events are especially important because they can change the comparison set overnight. When a company is moved from one industry group to another, historical trend lines may become harder to interpret, and relative performance rankings can shift even if the underlying business has not changed much. For that reason, investors need to know whether a move reflects a genuine shift in business mix, a change in reporting structure, or simply a taxonomy update by the classification provider. The practical question is not just where the company sits today, but whether its current label still captures the economic reality that will drive future results.

Classification systems are also used to build benchmarks, index products, and risk models. Portfolio managers measure active bets against sector weights, analysts compare returns on capital against industry medians, and risk teams estimate concentration by grouping holdings into common buckets. This creates useful discipline, but it can also encourage mechanical thinking if the labels are followed too rigidly. A business may be formally placed in one group while its most important operating sensitivities align more closely with another, which is why experienced investors often supplement official classifications with their own internal peer groups. Research on sectoral and industry definitions in other fields shows the same general principle: the usefulness of a classification depends on whether it captures the relevant economic distinctions, not merely whether it is tidy on paper [27].

That is why classification in practice is best understood as a layered process. The formal taxonomy provides consistency, but the analyst still has to decide which peer set is most informative for the question being asked. For valuation work, the right peers may be the firms with similar margins, reinvestment needs, and growth durability. For earnings analysis, the right peers may be the firms exposed to the same pricing cycle, input costs, or customer budget. For portfolio construction, the right peers may be the names that respond similarly to macro shocks. The label on the screen is useful, but the real work begins when the investor tests whether that label matches the economic terrain beneath it.

Peer groups, benchmarks, and relative performance

Peer groups are the practical bridge between classification and judgment. Once a company has been placed in the right sector and industry, the next question is not simply whether it is profitable, but whether it is profitable relative to the businesses it truly competes with. That comparison set is rarely the entire sector. A large-cap software platform, for example, may share a sector label with dozens of other technology firms, yet its economics may be far closer to a handful of subscription-based peers than to hardware vendors, IT services firms, or semiconductor producers. The right peer group narrows the field to companies with similar demand drivers, pricing behavior, capital intensity, and margin structure. Without that narrowing, valuation and operating metrics can be distorted by apples-to-oranges comparisons that tell the analyst more about classification labels than about business reality.

Benchmarks serve a different but equally important function. A peer group is the set of companies used for comparison; a benchmark is the reference line used to measure performance against a market, an industry, or an investment mandate. Some benchmarks are broad, such as a sector ETF, a style index, or a market-cap weighted industry index. Others are more customized, such as a hand-built basket of direct competitors or a portfolio-specific hurdle rate. The benchmark matters because it shapes the interpretation of results. A stock that rises 8% may look strong in isolation, but if its peer group rises 15% over the same period, the company has underperformed on a relative basis. Conversely, a business that declines during a weak market may still have outperformed if its peers fell harder. Relative performance is often the real signal investors are trying to detect: whether capital is flowing toward a group, whether the group is losing favor, or whether a company is gaining share inside a difficult environment.

This relative lens is especially useful because markets do not reward absolute quality in a vacuum. They reward quality that is better than expected, better than alternatives, or better than the rest of the field. A firm can have solid earnings, healthy cash flow, and disciplined capital allocation and still lag if its peer group is enjoying a stronger cycle, a faster growth rate, or a more favorable valuation rerating. The opposite also happens: a mediocre business can outperform if it sits in a temporarily favored niche or benefits from a rising tide across its industry. Relative performance therefore helps separate company-specific progress from group-level momentum. It also helps identify leadership. When a stock consistently outperforms its peers while maintaining stable margins and credible guidance, that strength often reflects more than market sentiment; it can signal superior execution, better positioning, or a more resilient business model.

For analysts, relative performance is not limited to price charts. It extends to revenue growth, margin trends, return on capital, leverage, cash conversion, and estimate revisions. A company may report slower growth than the market expects, yet still deserve a premium if its peer group is decelerating more sharply or if its margins are holding up better than competitors'. Likewise, a company may appear expensive on a simple multiple basis, but if its growth is faster, its balance sheet is cleaner, and its peer set is trading at even richer levels, the premium may be justified. In practice, relative analysis works best when it is layered: compare the company to direct peers, compare the peer group to the broader industry, and compare the industry to the market as a whole. Each layer answers a different question about whether the business is merely participating in a favorable environment or genuinely outperforming inside that environment.

The construction of peer groups requires judgment. Companies that appear similar on the surface may differ in the variables that matter most. Two retailers may both sell consumer goods, but one may be a high-turnover, low-margin operator with heavy store traffic while the other depends on premium pricing, online fulfillment, and a different seasonal pattern. Two banks may both be regional lenders, but one may have a commercial-heavy book, another a mortgage-heavy book, and a third a deposit franchise that gives it a structural funding advantage. The analyst must decide which characteristics drive the economic comparison. This is why peer groups should be defined by business model first and by label second. If the wrong peers are chosen, the resulting benchmark can reward the wrong behavior and hide the real source of risk.

Relative performance also reveals how investors are pricing uncertainty. When a group begins to outperform, the move may reflect improving fundamentals, but it may also reflect a shift in sentiment before the numbers fully change. That is why relative strength is often studied alongside earnings revisions and guidance trends. If a company's shares are outperforming while estimates are being revised upward and margins are stabilizing, the market may be recognizing a genuine improvement in earnings power. If the shares are outperforming without corresponding support in fundamentals, the move may be more fragile. In that sense, peer comparison is not just a ranking exercise. It is a way of testing whether the market's judgment is being confirmed by operating data or merely carried by momentum.

The most useful peer and benchmark work is disciplined rather than decorative. It does not ask whether a company is "good" in some abstract sense. It asks whether the company is better or worse than the businesses that define its economic neighborhood, and whether that difference is reflected in price. That is the point at which sector and industry analysis becomes actionable: not when a label is assigned, but when the label is used to locate the right comparisons, the right benchmark, and the right standard for relative performance.

Using market maps to narrow research efficiently

Market maps are most useful when they help an analyst decide where not to spend time. The equity universe is too large to study in a flat, undifferentiated way, so the first task is to reduce it to a smaller set of businesses with similar economic drivers. A well-built map does that by showing how sectors branch into industries and how those industries break into still narrower subindustries. The purpose is not to memorize labels for their own sake, but to identify where revenue sensitivity, margin structure, capital intensity, and competitive behavior are likely to be shared. Once that framework is in place, research becomes more efficient because the analyst can move from the broad question of "what kind of business is this?" to the more useful question of "which peers face the same operating conditions?"

Efficient narrowing begins with the sector level because it gives the first clue about the dominant forces at work. Some sectors are primarily shaped by consumer demand, others by business investment, regulation, commodity prices, or interest rates. That broad classification helps eliminate comparisons that look reasonable on the surface but are economically misleading. A payment processor and an industrial distributor may both be publicly traded and profitable, but they do not respond to the same drivers, and their financial statements should not be read through the same lens. By starting at the sector level, the analyst avoids wasting time on irrelevant comparables and can focus on the handful of variables most likely to explain performance.

The next filter is the industry group, where the real research savings begin. Within a sector, companies may share a broad label while still facing very different economics. An industry map helps separate businesses that are exposed to the same pricing environment, demand cycle, and cost structure from those that merely belong to the same administrative category. This is especially important when screening for valuation opportunities. A stock may look inexpensive relative to the sector but expensive relative to the industry, or vice versa. Without the map, the investor risks using a benchmark that is too broad to be meaningful. With it, the analyst can compare firms that are actually competing for the same customers, capital, or distribution channels.

Subindustry detail matters when the goal is to isolate the source of outperformance or weakness. In many cases, the most important differences are not captured by the sector label at all. Two companies can sit inside the same industry and still have very different exposure to cloud migration, subscription models, hardware refresh cycles, or regulatory change. The more precise the classification, the easier it becomes to determine whether a reported trend is company-specific or shared across a cluster of similar businesses. This is also where screening becomes more disciplined: instead of scanning hundreds of names, the analyst can focus on a narrow peer set that reflects the same product mix, customer base, and operating model.

Classification systems are most valuable when they are used as a research filter rather than as a substitute for judgment. A market map should not be treated as an immutable truth. Companies evolve, diversify, and sometimes straddle more than one economic category. That means the analyst must verify whether the label still matches the business reality. A firm may be classified in one place for administrative consistency, yet its earnings may now be driven by a different line of business. In that situation, the map still helps, but only if the investor recognizes that the classification is a starting point, not the final answer. The real task is to align the label with the company's current revenue sources, margin drivers, and competitive set.

Used properly, the map improves both speed and quality of research. It tells the analyst which financial statement line items deserve the most attention, which peer companies should be examined side by side, and which historical periods are most relevant for comparison. It also helps prevent false confidence from broad market narratives. A sector may be out of favor while a subindustry inside it is quietly improving, or a popular group may be masking deteriorating fundamentals in one pocket of the market. Recent descriptive work on listed firms emphasizes that valuation, liquidity, and risk indicators vary meaningfully across market segments, reinforcing the need to compare like with like rather than rely on broad averages [11].

The practical payoff is that the analyst reaches better questions faster. Instead of asking whether a company is simply "cheap" or "expensive," the research process becomes more precise: Is it cheap relative to the right peer group? Is its growth rate unusual for this subindustry? Are margins above or below the range implied by the industry structure? Is the market pricing in a temporary cycle or a lasting shift in fundamentals? A market map does not answer those questions on its own, but it sharpens them. That is what makes it an efficient research tool: it narrows the field before the deeper work begins, so the analyst spends time on the comparisons that actually matter.

Chapter 3: Reading the Economic Backdrop

Once the company and its competitive setting are identified, the next layer of analysis is the economic backdrop that can lift or restrain an entire group at once. Sectors do not respond evenly to the same macro conditions because their revenues, costs, and financing needs are tied to different parts of the economy. A change in growth, credit availability, labor pressure, or consumer demand can alter the earnings path of one industry while leaving another relatively untouched. This is why sector analysis requires more than a general view of "the economy" in the abstract; it requires reading the specific signals that matter for business activity and recognizing how those signals filter through to expectations, revisions, and valuation.

Key macro variables that move sectors

Sectors are moved by a small set of macro variables that alter demand, pricing, financing, and profitability at the same time. The most important are economic growth, interest rates, inflation, credit conditions, labor costs, commodity prices, and currency trends. Each one affects industries differently because each sector has its own mix of fixed costs, variable costs, leverage, and customer sensitivity. A change in the same macro variable can therefore strengthen one group while weakening another, even if the broader market appears to be moving in only one direction.

Economic growth is often the first variable investors watch because it influences the volume of goods and services that end markets can absorb. When growth accelerates, sectors tied to discretionary spending, capital investment, and industrial activity often benefit as customers become more willing to spend and businesses more willing to expand. When growth slows, those same sectors can see order delays, weaker pricing, and more cautious guidance. Defensive sectors, by contrast, often hold up better because their demand is less dependent on the pace of the economy. The key point is not simply whether GDP is rising or falling, but whether the pace of growth is changing enough to alter expectations for revenue and earnings.

Interest rates matter because they change both the cost of capital and the present value of future cash flows. Higher rates can pressure sectors that rely heavily on borrowing, refinancing, or long-duration growth assumptions. Real estate, utilities, and other capital-intensive groups often face a direct valuation headwind when discount rates rise, while banks and insurers may experience a more complex effect depending on the shape of the yield curve and the behavior of funding costs. Lower rates can ease financing stress and support valuation multiples, but they can also signal weaker growth, which may offset the benefit in cyclical sectors. Rate sensitivity is therefore not a one-dimensional story; it depends on whether the sector is being judged primarily on financing expense, asset valuation, or earnings momentum.

Inflation influences sectors through both revenue and cost channels. In some industries, firms can pass higher input costs on to customers fairly quickly, which can preserve margins or even improve reported sales growth in nominal terms. In others, pricing power is limited, and inflation becomes a margin squeeze. Food, energy, transportation, packaging, and labor-intensive services are especially exposed when costs rise faster than prices can be adjusted. Inflation also changes investor behavior by favoring businesses with hard assets, contractual pricing, or short inventory cycles over businesses whose margins depend on stable input costs and long production lead times. Analysis of inflation sensitivity should always distinguish between temporary price pass-through and true improvement in real profitability.

Credit conditions are another major driver because many sectors depend on the availability of financing, consumer borrowing, or working capital. When credit is easy, lenders extend more loans, consumers can finance large purchases, and companies can fund expansion with less immediate strain. That environment tends to support housing-related businesses, autos, private equity-backed firms, and other credit-dependent segments. When lending standards tighten, demand can weaken quickly even if headline economic data still looks acceptable. Sector analysis should therefore pay attention not only to policy rates, but also to spreads, underwriting standards, delinquency trends, and refinancing windows. A sector can look healthy until credit availability begins to contract, at which point earnings revisions often follow with a lag.

Labor costs affect sectors unevenly depending on how labor-intensive the business model is and how much pricing power management has. Restaurants, healthcare services, logistics, retail, and many consumer-facing businesses can see margins move sharply when wages rise faster than productivity. Firms with automation, software leverage, or high gross margins can absorb labor pressure more easily than firms that rely on large hourly workforces. Labor tightness can also influence service quality, turnover, and capacity utilization, which means the impact is not limited to reported expenses. In sectors where labor is both a cost and a constraint on growth, rising wages may increase revenue potential while simultaneously compressing margins, making the net effect harder to judge than a simple cost model suggests.

Commodity prices are especially important for sectors tied to extraction, transportation, manufacturing, and consumer staples. For producers of oil, metals, chemicals, and agricultural inputs, higher commodity prices can lift revenues and earnings quickly, though often with significant volatility. For users of those inputs, the same move can hurt margins unless prices can be passed through. This is why energy, materials, airlines, food producers, and packaged goods companies often react differently to the same commodity shock. Analysts also need to separate price moves caused by supply disruptions from those caused by demand growth, since the earnings implications are not identical. A supply-driven price spike may help producers immediately, while a demand-driven rise may signal stronger broad economic activity that supports a wider set of sectors.

Currency trends matter most for companies with international revenue, global supply chains, or foreign-denominated costs. A stronger domestic currency can reduce the translated value of overseas earnings and make exports less competitive, while a weaker currency can provide a tailwind to multinational firms that earn abroad and report in domestic terms. The effect is not uniform, however, because some companies benefit from imported inputs, while others are exposed to foreign sales but domestic costs. Currency moves can also change relative competitiveness within a sector, especially when peers have different geographic footprints. For that reason, currency analysis is less about forecasting exchange rates in isolation and more about identifying which businesses have natural hedges and which have direct exposure.

Applied general equilibrium research is useful here because it highlights a basic truth: sector outcomes are interconnected, and a policy or macro shock rarely stays confined to one line of business [4]. In market terms, that means the best sector analysis does not treat macro variables as abstract headlines. It traces the transmission path from the variable to demand, costs, financing, and valuation. The analyst's task is to ask which sectors are most exposed, which are partially insulated, and which may actually benefit from the same change that hurts others. That discipline turns macro data from a background narrative into an earnings framework.

Leading, lagging, and coincident indicators

Leading indicators are the signals that tend to change before the broader economy or a sector's earnings trend has fully turned. They are useful because markets do not wait for the reported data to confirm a shift; they often begin pricing the shift as soon as investors detect a change in demand, credit conditions, inventories, or expectations. In sector analysis, this matters because the first movement is often not in reported revenue or earnings, but in the variables that feed them. New orders, building permits, loan growth, purchasing manager surveys, commodity prices, and yield-curve movements can all hint that a sector is about to accelerate or slow long before that change appears in quarterly statements. Analysts use leading indicators to anticipate inflection points rather than merely describe what has already happened.

Lagging indicators, by contrast, confirm a move after it is already underway. Employment levels, corporate profits, delinquency rates, and inflation measures often fit this category because they reflect conditions that have already worked their way through the system. That does not make them less useful. In many industries, lagging indicators are the evidence that a thesis was right or wrong. A bank may see early signs of credit tightening in loan demand and spreads, but charge-offs and nonperforming assets may not rise until much later. A consumer company may experience softer traffic well before revenue growth visibly decelerates. Lagging data are important because they help investors verify whether an apparent shift in the environment is temporary noise or a durable change in fundamentals.

Coincident indicators sit in the middle. They move with the economy rather than clearly before or after it, so they are often the best read on current conditions. Industrial production, personal income, retail sales, and payrolls are common examples. For sector analysis, coincident indicators are valuable because they describe the present tense of the economy, which is where many earnings models need to anchor their assumptions. If a sector depends on current end-market activity, a coincident measure can help determine whether the business is operating in a healthy demand environment or merely benefiting from a lagged effect that will soon fade. In practice, analysts often combine coincident data with leading signals to distinguish between a stable trend and a trend that is already rolling over.

The real value of these categories is not in memorizing definitions, but in understanding how they interact. A leading indicator may turn positive while lagging indicators remain weak, and that gap can persist for months. During that period, investors who rely only on backward-looking data may miss the turn, while investors who rely only on leading data may become too early. Sector analysis requires balancing both. If housing starts improve, for example, that may be an early sign for building products, home improvement, and selected financials, but it does not mean every related company will report stronger results immediately. Inventory overhang, pricing pressure, or financing constraints can delay the translation from macro signal to earnings impact.

This timing gap is one reason sector cycles can look inconsistent to investors who examine only one indicator at a time. A sector may appear weak on reported earnings even while the forward-looking setup is improving. That can happen when management teams are still cutting production, clearing excess inventory, or absorbing higher input costs from a previous downturn. The opposite can also happen: a sector may post strong recent results while leading indicators have already begun to deteriorate. In that case, the numbers are not false, but they are stale. The market often notices the change before the income statement does, which is why sector analysis is partly an exercise in reading where the data sit in the cycle [39].

Different industries also emphasize different indicator sets. Cyclical industries such as autos, semiconductors, capital goods, and housing-related businesses often respond quickly to leading measures of demand, financing, and inventories. Defensive industries such as utilities, household staples, and certain healthcare segments may be more influenced by coincident measures of income, employment, and consumption stability. Commodity-linked businesses may require attention to both leading global demand signals and supply-side indicators such as production discipline, storage levels, and spot prices. The point is not that one category of indicator matters universally more than another, but that the relevant mix changes with the industry's economic exposure.

For analysts and investors, the practical discipline is to ask which indicator is most likely to move first, which one will confirm the move, and which one will reveal whether the move is durable. That sequence helps prevent the common mistake of overreacting to a single data point. A weak monthly survey may be a warning sign, but it is not the same as a confirmed earnings slowdown. Likewise, a strong current earnings report may reflect conditions that have already peaked. Sector work becomes stronger when it treats leading, lagging, and coincident indicators as parts of one timeline rather than as competing signals. The objective is not to find a perfect forecast, but to place each data point in the correct stage of the cycle and judge whether the market has already started to do the same.

Interest-rate and inflation sensitivity by sector

Interest rates and inflation do not affect every sector in the same way because they enter the earnings model through different channels. For some businesses, the main issue is the cost of borrowing. For others, it is the pace of consumer demand, the ability to pass through higher costs, or the present value investors assign to future cash flows. A sector with heavy capital needs and frequent refinancing will usually react more sharply to higher rates than a sector funded largely by internally generated cash. A sector with strong pricing power may offset inflation by raising prices, while a sector selling standardized products into competitive markets may absorb the cost in margins. The point is not simply that rates and inflation matter; it is that they change the economics of each sector in distinct ways.

Financials are the clearest example of how interest-rate sensitivity can be nuanced rather than one-directional. Banks, insurers, and asset managers all respond to rates, but not in identical fashion. For banks, the shape of the yield curve, deposit pricing, loan demand, and credit quality can matter as much as the level of short-term rates. Higher rates may improve net interest income if asset yields reprice faster than funding costs, yet they can also slow loan growth and raise default risk. Insurance companies may benefit from reinvestment opportunities on fixed-income portfolios, but higher rates can also affect the value of existing holdings and the demand for certain products. Financial sector analysis therefore requires a view of spread dynamics, funding structure, and asset-liability management rather than a simple assumption that "higher rates are good" or "higher rates are bad." Bank-sector crises have repeatedly shown how quickly funding conditions and risk management can overwhelm surface-level earnings trends [38].

Real estate, utilities, and other capital-intensive sectors typically show a more direct sensitivity to rates because their valuations and operating models are built around long-duration cash flows and heavy financing needs. When discount rates rise, the present value of future rent, toll, or regulated cash flow declines, even if the underlying business remains stable. At the same time, refinancing debt becomes more expensive, which can pressure funds from operations, coverage ratios, and dividend sustainability. Utilities may have partial protection through regulated returns and rate-base growth, but that does not eliminate sensitivity to financing costs. Real estate investment trusts may have lease escalators that help with inflation, yet they still face a higher hurdle when debt matures or when investors demand a larger yield premium over Treasuries.

Consumer sectors often respond first through demand rather than financing. In discretionary retail, restaurants, travel, and leisure, higher rates can reduce the willingness of households to spend on nonessential items, especially when borrowing costs rise on credit cards, auto loans, or mortgages. Inflation can cut in two directions here. If wage growth and spending power keep up, nominal sales may rise even as unit volume softens. If wages lag, households trade down, delay purchases, or shift toward lower-priced alternatives. Staples businesses are usually more insulated because demand is less elastic, but they are not immune: if inflation outpaces pricing power, margins can compress even when volumes hold up. In practice, the analyst has to separate unit demand, mix, and price realization rather than treat revenue growth as a single number.

Industrials and materials are often exposed to inflation through input costs, energy prices, freight, and labor. These sectors can sometimes pass through higher costs, but the timing matters. If cost inflation arrives quickly and customer contracts reset slowly, margins can be squeezed for several quarters. If inflation is accompanied by strong end-market demand, pricing may recover and even support earnings growth. Commodity-linked businesses are different again: for producers of oil, metals, chemicals, or agricultural inputs, inflation can improve realized prices and reported revenue, but it may also raise replacement costs, increase volatility, and distort comparisons with prior periods. In these sectors, inflation sensitivity is not a single beta; it is a set of exposures tied to input intensity, contract structure, and inventory timing.

Technology and communication services are often treated as “rate sensitive” because many of their valuations depend on cash flows expected far into the future. When discount rates rise, those distant cash flows are worth less in present-value terms, which can compress multiples even before earnings estimates change. This effect is strongest in businesses whose value rests on long-term growth rather than current profitability. Yet inflation can also matter operationally. Software firms with recurring subscriptions may have enough pricing power to offset cost pressures, while hardware and platform businesses exposed to global supply chains may face margin risk from components, logistics, or wages. The market often prices these groups as if valuation sensitivity were the only issue, but the operating sensitivity can be just as important.

The most useful way to analyze rate and inflation sensitivity is to ask four questions: how quickly do revenues reprice, how quickly do costs reprice, how much debt must be refinanced, and how sensitive is valuation to the discount rate? A sector with fast pricing power, low leverage, and short contract durations may handle inflation better than one with fixed pricing and high refinancing needs. A sector with stable current earnings may still be vulnerable if its valuation depends on long-duration growth assumptions. Inflation can also be a hidden source of earnings quality risk: reported revenue may look healthy while real volume stagnates, or margin expansion may reflect temporary price increases rather than durable efficiency. That is why sector analysis in a changing rate environment must connect macro conditions to the mechanics of the income statement, balance sheet, and valuation multiple at the same time.

How to translate economic data into sector expectations

Economic data becomes useful for sector analysis only when it is translated from broad headlines into specific earnings effects. A report showing stronger GDP growth, for example, does not automatically mean all sectors should rise. The analyst has to ask where the growth is coming from, which parts of the economy are receiving the incremental spending, and which industries are positioned to capture that demand. A pickup in household consumption may support retailers, payment processors, and select consumer discretionary names, while a rise in business investment may matter more to industrials, semiconductors, and capital equipment suppliers. The same macro release can therefore imply very different sector expectations depending on the composition of growth.

The first step is to connect each data point to the revenue engine of the sector. If the data reflects consumer demand, the relevant question is whether spending is broad-based or concentrated in necessities, services, or durable goods. If the data reflects manufacturing activity, the issue is whether new orders, inventories, and shipment trends are improving enough to support pricing and volume growth. If the data reflects credit conditions, the analyst should consider whether easier lending will expand loan growth, reduce default risk, or simply delay stress already building in weaker borrowers. This translation process turns macro information into an earnings hypothesis rather than a vague market impression.

It also helps to separate what is leading from what is merely confirming. Markets often react first to forward-looking measures such as purchasing manager surveys, consumer confidence, housing starts, lending standards, or commodity futures, because these variables can move before reported sales and earnings do. By contrast, payrolls, industrial production, and quarterly GDP often confirm a change that is already underway. That distinction matters because sector expectations should be built around the data that most directly alters the next several quarters of revenue, margins, and capital spending, not just the data that is easiest to observe after the fact. Textual analysis of corporate reporting has also shown that disclosure patterns and complexity can shift with regulation and incentives, which is a reminder that not all reported data is equally transparent or equally comparable across firms and jurisdictions [17].

Interest rates and inflation require an especially careful translation because they affect sectors through multiple channels at once. Higher rates can raise financing costs, depress valuation multiples, and slow interest-sensitive demand, but the magnitude of the effect depends on leverage, refinancing schedules, and customer behavior. Inflation can help firms with strong pricing power and flexible cost structures, while damaging companies that cannot pass through higher input costs quickly enough. For a capital-intensive business, inflation may increase replacement costs and squeeze returns on new investment; for a service business with limited physical assets, it may matter more through wages and customer churn. The key is not whether inflation is "good" or "bad" in the abstract, but which line items in the income statement and balance sheet are most exposed.

Credit data deserves special attention because it often reveals sector stress before earnings do. Tightening loan standards, rising funding costs, or weaker deposit retention can pressure banks even before charge-offs appear. In retail banking, customer switching behavior is a useful reminder that revenue durability depends not only on product pricing but also on retention, service quality, and the cost of replacing lost relationships [2]. A bank may report stable earnings while quietly facing deteriorating customer economics, especially if it is relying on short-term pricing tactics to preserve balances. In other sectors, similar logic applies through trade credit, supplier financing, or customer prepayments. When credit conditions tighten, the analyst should expect the weakest balance sheets, most cyclical demand profiles, and least loyal customer bases to show strain first.

Commodity prices and labor costs require another layer of interpretation because they can help one part of a sector while hurting another. A rise in input prices may support upstream producers but compress margins for downstream manufacturers and retailers. A decline in energy prices may relieve transportation, chemicals, and consumer spending, yet weaken producers and service firms tied to drilling activity. Likewise, rising wages can signal healthy labor demand, but they may hurt labor-intensive industries with limited pricing power. A useful practice is to identify whether the sector is a net buyer or net seller of the relevant input, then ask how quickly contracts, pricing models, and operating leverage transmit the change into earnings.

Macro translation becomes more reliable when the analyst builds a simple chain from data to behavior to financial result. Start with the economic signal, then identify the likely response from customers, suppliers, lenders, and competitors, and only then estimate the effect on revenue growth, margin direction, and capital intensity. A stronger housing report, for instance, may improve expectations for mortgage originators, homebuilders, building products, and insurers with property exposure, but the timing and magnitude will differ across each one because their revenue recognition, inventory positions, and financing needs are not the same. The same discipline applies to employment, trade, manufacturing, and inflation data: the point is not to memorize which sector "likes" a statistic, but to understand the mechanism by which that statistic changes the economics of the business.

In practice, sector expectations should be phrased as conditional statements rather than fixed predictions. If growth accelerates and credit remains available, then cyclical sectors with operating leverage should see better earnings revisions. If inflation cools and rates stabilize, then long-duration growth sectors may benefit from improved valuation support and easier funding conditions. If consumer sentiment weakens while wage growth slows, then discretionary spending may soften before the broader economy does. This language keeps the analysis anchored to cause and effect, which is the real purpose of reading economic data in a sector framework: not to forecast the entire market with one indicator, but to identify which groups are most likely to experience improving or deteriorating fundamentals next.

Chapter 4: Understanding Industry Structure and Competitive Forces

Once the broad economic setting has been identified, the next question is how much of a company's outcome is determined by the structure of the industry itself. Some businesses operate in fields where profitability is naturally constrained by intense rivalry, limited differentiation, or persistent price pressure; others benefit from structures that allow stronger returns to endure for longer periods. This is why industry analysis is not just about naming competitors, but about understanding the economic rules that govern them. The same revenue trend can have very different implications depending on how concentrated the market is, how easily customers can switch, and how much bargaining power sits with suppliers, buyers, or intermediaries.

Industry attractiveness and profitability

Industry attractiveness is the starting point for judging whether a business can earn durable profits, but it should not be confused with a simple popularity contest. An industry may look exciting because it is growing quickly, yet still be unattractive if competition is intense, switching costs are low, and new entrants can flood the market. Another industry may grow slowly and appear dull, but still support strong profitability because a few firms control distribution, customers face high switching costs, or the business requires specialized assets that are difficult to replicate. The key question is not whether the industry is large or fashionable, but whether its structure allows companies to keep enough of the value they create.

Profitability in this setting is not just about reported net income. It is the result of how much pricing power a company has, how much of its revenue it must spend to acquire and retain customers, how much capital it must reinvest to keep operating, and how much of the industry's economics are captured by suppliers, labor, distributors, or customers. A highly attractive industry tends to support higher and more stable returns on capital because firms can earn acceptable margins without constantly sacrificing price or taking on excessive risk. In less attractive industries, profits are often competed away quickly, and even strong operators can struggle to sustain returns above their cost of capital.

One reason industry attractiveness matters so much is that it helps explain why similar companies can produce very different earnings quality. In a favorable structure, revenue may be more recurring, customer retention may be stronger, and margins may be less exposed to sudden price wars. In a weak structure, earnings may depend on temporary demand spikes, aggressive promotions, or a brief imbalance between supply and demand. That distinction matters because investors often mistake a cyclical upswing for a durable improvement in economics. A business can report a period of impressive profitability while operating in an industry where those profits are unlikely to last once competition normalizes.

Customer behavior is central to this analysis. When customers can switch easily, firms must compete harder on price, service, or product features, and that pressure usually compresses margins. Research in retail banking, for example, has shown that customer retention can create meaningful revenue benefits and cost savings because acquiring replacement customers is expensive and loyalty reduces churn [2]. The same principle applies across many industries: the more difficult it is for customers to leave, the more room a firm has to preserve profitability. High retention does not guarantee strong margins, but it often supports them by lowering sales friction and reducing the need for constant discounting.

Industry attractiveness also depends on the balance between supply and demand. If capacity can expand quickly, any period of strong demand may invite new entrants or aggressive expansion from existing competitors, which can cap profits. If capacity is constrained by regulation, capital intensity, technical expertise, or scarce inputs, profitability can remain stronger for longer because the market cannot be flooded as easily. This is why analysts pay attention not only to current earnings, but also to the structure of the market behind those earnings. A profitable year is more meaningful when the industry has barriers that make it hard for competitors to chase the same returns.

Capital intensity deserves special attention because it changes the quality of profit. Two industries may show similar operating margins, yet one may require far more investment in plants, inventories, networks, or technology to sustain those margins. In that case, the apparent profitability may not translate into attractive returns on invested capital. The more capital an industry consumes to generate each incremental dollar of revenue, the more demanding the earnings model becomes. Investors should therefore ask whether profits are being produced efficiently or merely reported at the top of the income statement while the balance sheet absorbs the real cost.

Industry structure also influences how durable profitability can be across the cycle. In some industries, strong demand leads quickly to overcapacity, which then triggers price competition and margin compression. In others, demand growth can be absorbed without a rapid collapse in pricing because the market is concentrated or because customers value reliability, brand, or integration more than the lowest price. Applied general equilibrium analysis is often used in economics to study how sector-level outcomes change when supply, demand, and policy interact across a broader system [4]. For investors, the practical lesson is similar: profitability should be judged in relation to the forces that shape the entire industry, not just the latest quarter.

That is why industry attractiveness is best treated as a range rather than a label. No industry is permanently excellent or permanently poor. Competitive conditions evolve, technology changes cost structures, regulation shifts bargaining power, and customer preferences alter the basis of competition. A disciplined analyst looks for the features that support above-average profits: differentiated products, loyal customers, limited substitution, disciplined capital allocation, and barriers that slow new competition. When those features are absent, even a business with strong execution may find it difficult to convert sales growth into lasting profitability.

Competitive forces and their impact on margins

Competitive forces shape margins by determining how much pricing power a company really has, how much of its cost structure can be passed through, and how quickly attractive returns are competed away. In industries with intense rivalry, even firms with strong brands may find that price competition, promotional spending, and customer churn steadily compress operating margins. In more protected industries, the same level of demand can translate into much higher profitability because firms do not need to sacrifice price to defend share. The important point is that margins are not just the result of internal efficiency; they are also a reflection of the rules of competition that govern the industry.

The most immediate force is rivalry among existing competitors. When several firms sell similar products and customers can compare them easily, the market tends to reward the lowest price, the fastest delivery, or the most aggressive promotion. That dynamic often forces companies to spend more on advertising, rebates, sales incentives, or service upgrades simply to hold their position. Over time, those added expenses become embedded in the income statement and show up as thinner gross and operating margins. A business may still grow revenue in such an environment, but growth can come at the cost of profitability if every incremental sale requires more discounting or support.

Customer switching behavior is central to this process. When buyers can move freely from one supplier to another, the seller has little room to raise prices or reduce service quality without losing volume. Research on retail banking has shown that the longer a bank retains a customer, the greater the revenue and cost savings from that relationship, which helps explain why switching costs matter so much for profitability [2]. The same principle applies across sectors: the easier it is for customers to leave, the more a company must spend to keep them, and the more margins become exposed to competitive pressure. Low switching costs usually mean that reported growth is less durable and that margin expansion is harder to sustain.

Threat from new entrants also affects margins by changing the balance between supply and demand. When capital requirements are modest, distribution is accessible, and products are easy to replicate, new competitors can enter quickly and force incumbents to defend share. That often leads to excess capacity, discounting, and a lower ceiling on industry returns. By contrast, industries with high entry barriers can preserve margins because new firms cannot easily match the scale, brand, technology, regulation, or customer relationships of established leaders. The result is not simply fewer competitors, but a more stable pricing environment in which margins are less likely to be eroded by constant imitation.

Substitute products create another margin constraint. A company may appear to have a strong position within its direct peer group, yet still face pressure if customers can solve the same problem through a different product category. Substitutes limit pricing power because buyers always have an alternative benchmark. If the alternative becomes cheaper, more convenient, or technologically superior, the original industry may be forced to lower prices or add features without receiving full compensation. This is why margin analysis should not stop at direct competitors. It must also ask what other products or services can satisfy the same customer need and how easily those substitutes can be adopted.

Supplier and buyer power can tighten margins from both ends of the income statement. Strong suppliers can raise input costs faster than firms can pass them through, especially when a company depends on a concentrated set of vendors or specialized components. Strong buyers, on the other hand, can demand lower prices, better terms, or more customization, shifting economics away from the seller. In industries where large customers account for a meaningful share of revenue, margins can be especially vulnerable because the buyer's negotiating leverage is concentrated and repeated every contract cycle. The more dependent a company is on a few suppliers or a few customers, the less control it has over its own profitability.

These competitive forces matter not only for current margins, but also for the quality of margin expansion. A company can widen margins temporarily through cost cuts, underinvestment, or favorable pricing conditions, but the more durable question is whether the industry structure supports those margins over time. If competition is fierce, a high margin may invite imitation, new capacity, or aggressive price response. If the industry has disciplined structure, the same margin level may be sustainable and even conservative. Applied sector analysis therefore treats margins as a signal of industry economics, not just management execution. It asks whether profitability is being earned because the business is genuinely advantaged, or whether it is merely benefiting from a temporary pause in competitive pressure.

Barriers to entry, scale, and network effects

Barriers to entry determine how easily new competitors can enter an industry and challenge existing firms. When entry is simple and inexpensive, attractive profits tend to draw in new players, and those profits are often competed away faster than investors expect. When entry requires specialized technology, regulatory approval, exclusive distribution, large upfront capital, or a trusted brand built over many years, incumbents are better protected. For the analyst, the key question is not whether an industry has competitors, but whether those competitors can realistically replicate the assets, relationships, or expertise that support current returns on capital. A business may look expensive on a conventional multiple and still be reasonably valued if the industry structure makes those returns unusually durable.

In practice, barriers to entry often show up in the financial statements before they are obvious in the market narrative. Stable gross margins, disciplined pricing, and limited promotional pressure can indicate that incumbents are not being forced into destructive competition. High customer retention, low churn, and repeat purchasing patterns can also signal that a newcomer would have to spend heavily just to win business away from established firms. In banking, for example, customer switching costs and relationship depth matter because the longer a customer stays, the more revenue and cost advantages the bank can accumulate [2]. That does not make the industry risk-free, but it does help explain why some financial businesses can sustain profitability even when the broader environment is competitive.

Scale is a separate but related force. A company with greater scale may buy inputs more cheaply, spread fixed costs over a larger revenue base, invest more heavily in technology, and support a broader sales or service network than smaller rivals. This can create a cost advantage that is difficult for entrants to match. Scale also matters because it can change the economics of growth itself: the larger the business, the more efficiently it may be able to add customers, process transactions, or serve a wider geography without a proportional rise in overhead. In sectors where production, logistics, compliance, or distribution require substantial fixed costs, the largest firms often enjoy the widest operating leverage. That advantage can be powerful, but it is not automatic; scale only becomes a moat when it translates into lower unit costs, stronger pricing power, or better customer acquisition economics.

For investors, the danger is assuming that size alone guarantees protection. Large firms can become slower, more bureaucratic, or more exposed to disruption if their scale is tied to outdated systems or a fading business model. The more useful question is whether scale is reinforcing the company's economics or merely making it bigger. A business that can reinvest at attractive rates because scale lowers its cost structure deserves a different valuation framework from a business that has grown large but must keep spending simply to defend its position. In some industries, scale also creates a self-reinforcing cycle: lower costs allow lower prices or better service, which attracts more customers, which further improves cost efficiency. When that cycle is present, analysts should be cautious about extrapolating competitive entry too easily.

Network effects are even more distinctive. They occur when a product or platform becomes more valuable as more people use it, which can create a powerful winner-take-most dynamic. Payment networks, marketplaces, communication platforms, and certain software ecosystems can all benefit from this pattern. The value to each participant rises as the network grows, making it harder for a new entrant to persuade users to switch to a smaller, less active alternative. In these cases, competitive advantage is not just about lower costs or better branding; it is about the structure of demand itself. Once a network reaches critical mass, the industry can become unusually sticky, and the leading firm may enjoy sustained growth, high margins, and strong cash generation for a prolonged period.

Network effects should still be examined carefully rather than accepted as a slogan. Not every business with many users has a true network effect, and not every network effect is strong enough to protect profits indefinitely. The analyst should ask whether each new user actually increases the value of the platform for existing users, whether multi-homing is common, and whether customers can shift to a rival without losing much utility. If switching is easy, then the network may be more fragile than it first appears. Where the network is real, however, it can meaningfully raise barriers to entry because a challenger must overcome both the incumbent's installed base and the momentum of user adoption. That is why industries with strong network effects often deserve premium valuation ranges, provided the economics are not being eroded by regulation, commoditization, or technological change.

These three forces often interact. Barriers to entry can protect the market position that scale then strengthens, while scale can help a platform or service deepen its network effects. The reverse is also possible: low barriers to entry can prevent scale advantages from becoming durable, and weak network effects can leave a formerly dominant business exposed once customer behavior changes. For sector and industry analysis, the practical task is to identify which force matters most in a given industry and how visible it is in the numbers. A business with strong margins, limited churn, and consistent reinvestment opportunities may be operating in a structurally favorable terrain. A business with thin margins, easy entry, and no meaningful switching costs may be fighting in a much harsher landscape, even if its recent results look temporarily strong.

How industry structure shapes valuation ranges

Industry structure sets the outer boundaries of valuation long before a single company-specific assumption is entered into a model. Investors often talk about "cheap" and "expensive" stocks as if those labels were absolute, but in practice they are relative to the economics of the industry. A business operating in a field with durable pricing power, recurring demand, and limited rivalry can justify a higher earnings multiple than a company in a fragmented market where customers switch easily and margins are repeatedly pressured. The market is not simply paying for current earnings; it is paying for the likelihood that those earnings can persist, expand, or be defended when conditions change.

That is why two firms with similar reported profits may deserve very different valuation ranges. In a concentrated industry, the leading players may enjoy scale advantages, brand strength, or network effects that make their cash flows more predictable. In a more competitive industry, the same level of profit may be less durable because rivals can copy features, undercut prices, or absorb market share with little friction. When the competitive structure is harsh, investors usually demand a lower multiple to compensate for the risk that today's margins will not survive. When the structure protects returns, the market is often willing to capitalize those returns at a richer level.

Switching costs are one of the clearest examples of how structure shapes valuation. When customers face meaningful operational disruption, retraining, integration expense, or relationship risk by changing suppliers, the incumbent's revenue base becomes stickier and the earnings stream more valuable. Research on retail banking found that the longer a bank can retain a customer, the greater the revenue and cost savings from that relationship [2]. That logic extends well beyond banking. A business with sticky customers can often sustain higher margins, lower acquisition expense, and more dependable renewal rates, all of which support a broader valuation range than a business that must continually "re-earn" each sale.

Barriers to entry matter just as much. If new competitors can enter with modest capital, little regulation, and no special distribution advantage, any attractive profit pool tends to attract fresh supply. As supply increases, pricing weakens, returns normalize, and valuation multiples compress. By contrast, industries protected by regulation, proprietary technology, scarce licenses, strong brands, or deep infrastructure can preserve excess returns for longer periods. The market recognizes that distinction by assigning a premium to earnings it believes are shielded from rapid imitation. This is one reason why a company with modest growth but high structural protection can trade at a higher multiple than a faster-growing company in a crowded field.

Capital intensity also shapes the range of reasonable valuations. Businesses that must continually reinvest heavily in plants, networks, inventory, or maintenance consume more of their operating cash flow just to stand still. Even if reported earnings look healthy, the portion available to owners may be lower after necessary reinvestment. That reduces the attractiveness of the earnings stream and tends to limit the multiple investors are willing to pay. Asset-light businesses, by contrast, can convert a larger share of revenue into free cash flow, which often leads to higher valuation ranges if growth is sustainable. The key is not simply how much a company earns, but how much capital it must deploy to keep earning it.

Industry structure also influences the range of acceptable valuation by affecting forecast confidence. Where demand is stable, customer behavior is predictable, and competitive responses are muted, analysts can model future cash flows with greater conviction. Lower uncertainty usually supports a higher multiple because less of the company's value depends on heroic assumptions. Where demand is cyclical, pricing is volatile, or the industry is exposed to policy and commodity shocks, a wider range of outcomes is appropriate. The market then discounts not only the level of earnings but the probability that those earnings could swing sharply. In sectors facing policy transition, for example, structural uncertainty can be as important as current profitability in determining the valuation ceiling [51].

This does not mean that all highly competitive industries deserve low multiples or that all protected industries deserve high ones. The valuation range is shaped by the interaction of structure, growth, and capital allocation. A difficult industry can still produce an attractive stock if a company is taking share, improving its cost position, or exiting low-return activities. A strong industry can still disappoint if management overpays for growth or wastes a favorable position with poor capital discipline. But even in those cases, the industry sets the starting point. It tells the analyst whether to expect a narrow band of normal returns, a premium for resilience, or a discount for fragility. Valuation is therefore less about labeling a stock expensive or cheap in isolation and more about asking what kind of business economics the market is being asked to capitalize.

Chapter 5: Sector Cycles, Industry Cycles, and Market Timing

Market timing in sector analysis begins with the recognition that industries do not move through the economy in a straight line. Their earnings, valuations, and investor sentiment tend to rise and fall in patterns that are tied to shifting demand, credit conditions, inventories, and expectations. Those patterns are not random, but neither are they perfectly predictable. They are shaped by how quickly firms can adjust capacity, how much pricing power they possess, and how sensitive their customers are to changes in the broader environment. Financing conditions can also amplify these swings, since sectors with more reliance on external capital often experience sharper changes in behavior when liquidity tightens or loosens [52].

The anatomy of a business cycle

The business cycle is not just a line on an economic chart. It is the shifting environment in which firms hire, borrow, produce, price, and report results. At its core, the cycle reflects changes in demand, credit availability, inventories, labor conditions, and confidence. Those forces do not move in perfect unison, which is why different industries often experience the same macro phase in very different ways. A manufacturer may feel the cycle through order flow and inventory swings, while a bank feels it through loan growth, funding costs, and credit quality, and a consumer-facing business feels it through traffic, basket size, and promotional intensity.

The anatomy of a business cycle begins with expansion. In the early part of an expansion, demand is improving from a weak base, capacity is usually underused, and firms can often grow without immediately facing severe cost pressure. This is the phase in which operating leverage can become powerful because fixed costs are already in place, so incremental revenue falls more cleanly to the bottom line. Balance sheets also tend to repair in this stage as cash flow improves and credit conditions ease. Industries that were previously constrained by caution, such as discretionary retail, travel, industrials, and financials, often begin to recover before the broader economic data looks fully healthy.

As expansion matures, the cycle enters a phase where growth remains solid but the easy gains have already been captured. Capacity tightens, labor becomes more expensive, and suppliers gain bargaining power. Companies that were once able to pass through higher costs with little resistance begin to encounter more friction. This is often when margins peak. Revenue may still rise, but the rate of improvement in earnings starts to slow because costs, competition, and capital spending become more demanding. Investors who focus only on the headline growth rate can miss the fact that the quality of that growth is deteriorating. A business can be selling more and still be moving into a less favorable part of the cycle.

Late-cycle conditions are often defined less by outright weakness than by strain. Inflationary pressure, tighter monetary policy, and more selective lending can all compress the room for error. Firms with heavy debt loads, short refinancing windows, or weak pricing power become more vulnerable because the cost of capital rises just as operating conditions become less forgiving. This is one reason financing cycles matter so much. Research on pledgeability and industry liquidity shows that firms' debt choices and subsequent performance are tied to how easily cash flows can be controlled and financed within their industry setting [52]. In practical terms, the late cycle tends to reward businesses with resilient cash generation and punish those that depend on abundant credit or optimistic assumptions.

Recessionary phases are usually marked by falling demand, inventory correction, and a sharper separation between strong and weak balance sheets. Companies with essential products, recurring revenue, or defensive demand often hold up better, but even these businesses can face valuation pressure if investors expect the downturn to last. Cyclical industries typically see the most dramatic earnings declines because volume falls, pricing weakens, and fixed costs are spread over fewer units. Yet the market often begins to recover before the recession is over, because equity prices discount the future rather than simply reporting the present. That is why cycle analysis is as much about expectations as it is about current data.

For sector analysis, the important point is that each phase changes the relative attractiveness of industries. Early-cycle environments often favor groups tied to renewed spending, restocking, and credit normalization. Mid-cycle conditions can support broader participation, but especially businesses with pricing power, steady demand, and efficient capital use. Late-cycle conditions usually shift attention toward quality, cash flow, and balance sheet strength. Recessionary periods tend to reward defensives, but they can also create opportunities in high-quality cyclicals if the market has already priced in a severe contraction. The same company may look expensive in one phase and cheap in another because the earnings base itself is moving.

Cycle analysis also requires attention to the internal mechanics of a business, not just the external macro setting. Inventory levels, customer prebuying, backlog, utilization rates, and wage pressure can all reveal where an industry sits in the cycle before reported earnings fully show it. In some sectors, order growth leads revenue by months; in others, contract backlogs or renewal rates provide the better signal. The analyst's task is to identify which operating variables move first, which ones lag, and which ones are most likely to reverse when conditions change. That is what turns the business cycle from a broad economic concept into a usable framework for judging earnings durability, margin risk, and valuation discipline.

Early-cycle, mid-cycle, late-cycle, and recessionary behavior

Sector behavior changes materially as the business cycle moves from expansion to slowdown because the sources of earnings growth, margin pressure, and investor preference are not constant. In an early-cycle environment, demand is usually recovering from a prior contraction, inventories are lean, credit conditions are improving, and confidence is rebuilding from depressed levels. That combination tends to favor businesses that are highly sensitive to a rebound in activity, especially those tied to industrial production, consumer discretionary spending, housing, and financial intermediation. The market often rewards these groups before the economic data look fully healthy, because investors are looking through the first phase of recovery toward the acceleration in sales and earnings that typically follows.

Early-cycle leadership is often driven by operating leverage. When revenue begins to recover from a low base, fixed costs are spread over a larger sales base, and profits can rise faster than sales. That is why cyclical industries can produce sharp earnings rebounds even if the macro backdrop still feels uncertain. At the same time, the market usually becomes more willing to pay for stocks that were previously discounted for recession risk. Credit spreads may narrow, banks may see better loan growth and lower loss provisioning, and companies with exposure to capital spending can benefit as customers restart deferred projects. This is also the phase in which macro uncertainty begins to decline from crisis levels, even if it remains elevated relative to normal [58].

Mid-cycle behavior is different because the recovery is no longer just a rebound from weakness; it becomes a more mature expansion in which growth is broader, capacity utilization is higher, and pricing power begins to matter more than simple volume recovery. In this phase, investors often shift toward companies that can sustain earnings growth without relying on a dramatic macro tailwind. Quality, balance sheet strength, and disciplined capital allocation become more important, because the easy gains from cyclical recovery have already been captured. Sectors with steadier demand and more visible cash generation can perform well alongside cyclical groups, especially if the expansion is not yet threatening inflation or forcing the central bank into a more restrictive stance.

Late-cycle conditions usually bring a different set of pressures. Labor markets tighten, input costs rise, inventories can become less manageable, and central banks may lean against inflation with tighter policy. As financing becomes more expensive and growth becomes harder to sustain, investors often become more selective about earnings quality. Companies that relied on easy credit, aggressive expansion, or weak competitive discipline may begin to show cracks in margins or cash flow. Late-cycle leadership often shifts toward businesses with pricing power, stable demand, and lower sensitivity to borrowing costs. Defensive sectors may begin to outperform on a relative basis, not necessarily because their absolute growth is strong, but because their earnings are less exposed to a slowdown in economic momentum.

Recessionary behavior tends to compress the range of outcomes across most sectors, but it does not affect all industries equally. Demand weakens, customers delay purchases, credit losses rise, and management teams often cut costs in response to falling visibility. Cyclical sectors usually experience the sharpest earnings declines because their revenues fall just as fixed costs remain in place. In contrast, defensive sectors such as utilities, consumer staples, and some health care businesses often see less severe deterioration because their products and services are less discretionary. Even so, recession does not automatically guarantee safety for every company in a defensive sector; leverage, reimbursement pressure, regulation, and input-cost inflation can still damage margins and cash flow.

The important analytical point is that cycle phase affects both fundamentals and valuation at the same time. In early-cycle periods, the market may assign higher multiples to businesses whose earnings are still depressed but likely to recover quickly. In late-cycle and recessionary periods, those same names can de-rate as investors become less willing to pay for earnings that appear vulnerable to a slowdown. Meanwhile, companies with steadier earnings streams may command a premium precisely because their cash flows look more reliable when uncertainty rises. The valuation spread between cyclical and defensive groups is therefore not just a matter of sentiment; it reflects changing expectations about the durability of earnings under different macro conditions.

For sector analysis, the practical challenge is to distinguish between temporary cycle effects and structural changes in industry economics. A downturn can make a strong business look weak if its earnings are temporarily compressed by inventory destocking, delayed purchases, or higher credit losses. A recovery can make a mediocre business look strong if it is simply benefiting from a rebound in demand rather than any lasting improvement in competitive position. That is why cycle analysis should be paired with an assessment of margin structure, balance-sheet resilience, and industry positioning. The same sector can move from leadership to laggard status as the cycle matures, and the companies best positioned in one phase are not always the winners in the next.

Cyclical versus defensive sectors

Cyclical sectors are the parts of the market whose earnings are tightly linked to the pace of economic activity, credit creation, inventory rebuilding, and discretionary spending. When growth accelerates, these businesses often see revenue, margins, and sentiment improve together. When growth slows, the same sensitivity that helped them in the upswing can quickly become a source of pressure. Defensive sectors, by contrast, are supported by demand that is less dependent on the business cycle. Their products and services tend to be purchased regardless of whether the economy is expanding or contracting, so their earnings usually fluctuate less, even if their stocks are not immune to market-wide declines.

The distinction matters because investors often confuse stability with safety and volatility with risk. A cyclical business can be financially strong, well managed, and competitively advantaged, yet still report uneven results because its end markets are tied to broader conditions. A defensive business can offer steadier earnings, but that steadiness may already be reflected in a higher valuation, leaving less room for disappointment. The analyst's task is not to ask which type is "better," but to identify which type of exposure is being purchased and whether that exposure fits the current phase of the cycle, the investor's time horizon, and the portfolio's existing composition.

What makes a sector cyclical is not simply that its stock price moves around a lot. The key issue is whether demand, pricing, and profitability rise and fall with the economy. Consumer discretionary, industrials, materials, and many energy businesses are classic examples because their results often depend on capital spending, housing activity, freight volumes, commodity demand, or household willingness to spend beyond essentials. In these sectors, small changes in demand can produce large changes in earnings because fixed costs are meaningful and operating leverage is high. That leverage works both ways: profits can expand rapidly in an upswing and contract sharply when volumes weaken.

Defensive sectors are defined less by excitement than by persistence. Consumer staples, utilities, health care, and parts of communication and infrastructure-related businesses often enjoy more stable demand because customers continue to buy, consume, or use the service through different economic environments. Some of these businesses still face pricing pressure, regulation, reimbursement risk, or input-cost volatility, so "defensive" does not mean risk-free. It means that the primary source of demand is less discretionary and less sensitive to swings in confidence or income. In practice, that often leads to flatter revenue paths, more predictable cash flow, and valuation multiples that reflect the market's willingness to pay for consistency.

The market usually prices these groups differently at different stages of the cycle. Early in an expansion, investors often favor cyclicals because earnings are recovering from depressed levels and the market is looking for acceleration. Later in the cycle, as growth becomes more mature and margins begin to face pressure, capital may rotate toward defensives as investors seek durability and protection. This rotation is not mechanical, and it is rarely clean. Some cyclical sectors can continue to outperform well into a late-cycle environment if supply remains tight or pricing power is unusually strong. Likewise, a defensive sector can lag badly if it is expensive, if rates rise sharply, or if investors are willing to pay up for faster growth elsewhere.

This is why sector labels should be treated as starting points, not final judgments. Two companies in the same broad sector can have very different cycle exposure depending on their customer mix, contract structure, geographic footprint, and capital intensity. A software business with recurring subscriptions may behave more defensively than a hardware supplier tied to corporate capital spending. A health care company with recurring prescriptions may be steadier than a device maker dependent on elective procedures. The correct question is not merely where a company sits on the classification map, but how much of its revenue and margin profile is exposed to discretionary demand, financing conditions, and inventory cycles.

For analysts, the practical value of the cyclical-versus-defensive distinction is that it improves interpretation. A slowdown in sales is more alarming for a cyclical business if the broader backdrop is already weakening, but less alarming for a defensive business if the decline reflects temporary pricing or mix effects. A margin compression episode in a cyclical sector may be the natural result of lower volume and less favorable fixed-cost absorption, while the same margin decline in a defensive sector may point to competitive pressure or a structural cost problem. Research on market behavior also shows that investor preferences can shift meaningfully between value and growth styles across different market regimes, reinforcing the idea that sector and style leadership are not fixed but responsive to the environment [64].

The most useful habit is to ask what must be true for the business model to perform well. If the answer depends on rising employment, expanding credit, higher commodity prices, or sustained capital spending, the business is likely cyclical. If the answer depends more on recurring consumption, regulated demand, or non-discretionary usage, it is likely defensive. That distinction does not determine whether the stock is attractive, but it does determine how the earnings should be forecast, how much confidence to place in current margins, and how much patience the investor will need when the cycle turns.

Practical timing signals for investors and traders

Practical timing signals are most useful when they translate broad sector and industry behavior into something an investor can observe before earnings reports confirm the move. The point is not to predict every turn with precision. It is to recognize when the balance of evidence is shifting from expansion to deceleration, from contraction to recovery, or from leadership to vulnerability. In sector analysis, timing is usually less about a single dramatic signal than about a cluster of smaller clues that begin to align. Price action, revisions, inventory behavior, credit conditions, and management commentary can all point in the same direction before the financial statements catch up.

One of the clearest signals is relative performance. When a sector begins to outperform the broad market while the underlying economy is still uncertain, it often means investors are anticipating better earnings conditions ahead. That can happen in the early stages of a recovery, when cyclical groups start to lead because demand is stabilizing and expectations are still low. The reverse is also informative. When a previously strong sector begins to lag even though headline fundamentals still look acceptable, the market may be discounting a future slowdown in margins, volumes, or pricing power. Relative strength and relative weakness matter because markets usually price change before the change is visible in reported results.

Another useful signal is the direction of earnings revisions. Analysts tend to revise estimates after a trend has already become visible in orders, pricing, or cost data, so the revision cycle itself can function as a timing tool. A sector with rising forward estimates, stable guidance, and positive surprise frequency is often in a more favorable phase than one in which estimates are being cut across the group. What matters most is not whether one company beats or misses by a small amount, but whether the pattern is broad enough to suggest a real shift in the industry backdrop. A wave of upward revisions across peers usually carries more information than a single standout report.

Inventory and channel indicators are especially important in industries tied to physical goods. When inventories are lean and demand is improving, companies can often raise prices, restore margins, and run production more efficiently. When inventories build faster than sell-through, the opposite tends to happen: discounting increases, margins compress, and future orders can weaken as customers work down excess stock. This is why investors and traders watch distributor commentary, days inventory outstanding, backlog trends, and channel checks so closely. These data points often reveal whether a sector is entering a period of replenishment or liquidation long before revenue growth fully reflects it.

Credit conditions provide another timing layer, particularly for sectors that depend on financing, consumer borrowing, or capital spending. Easier credit can support housing, autos, commercial investment, and other rate-sensitive groups, while tighter credit can restrain them even when demand appears healthy on the surface. In practice, the signal is not just whether rates are rising or falling, but whether lending standards are tightening, refinancing is becoming more expensive, or default expectations are deteriorating. Political and policy risk can also matter here, since shifts in regulation, taxation, or government priorities can alter sector prospects quickly [70]. For that reason, timing signals should include not only macro data but also the policy environment that shapes access to capital and the cost of doing business.

Management guidance and conference-call language can also be revealing, but only when read carefully. Words such as “normalize,” “stabilize,” “headwinds,” “seasonality,” and “cautious” often matter less in isolation than in the pattern they form across several companies in the same industry. If multiple firms begin to describe the same pressure on demand, pricing, or customer budgets, that repetition is often more meaningful than any one company's explanation. Similarly, when management teams start talking about improving conversion, better order flow, or easing cost pressures, the shift may indicate that the industry is moving out of a difficult phase. Financial statement analysis is most effective when it is paired with this kind of qualitative reading, because the numbers and the narrative often turn at different speeds [46].

For traders, timing signals often need to be compressed into a shorter horizon. That means giving greater weight to price momentum, earnings surprises, volatility, and near-term revisions. A group that breaks out on strong volume after a period of underperformance may be signaling a change in institutional sponsorship. A sector that reacts weakly to good news may be telling a different story: expectations were too high, positioning was crowded, or the market is already looking past the current quarter. Traders also pay attention to dispersion within a group. When leaders continue to outperform laggards by a wide margin, the industry may still be healthy; when the entire group weakens together, the problem is often structural rather than company-specific.

For investors with a longer horizon, the timing question is less about entry on a specific day and more about whether the sector is moving into a favorable part of its earnings cycle. That requires patience and discipline. A sector can look cheap for a long time if its fundamentals are still deteriorating, just as an expensive sector can stay expensive when its growth and margins are compounding faster than expected. The most reliable timing signals therefore combine valuation with evidence of inflection: improving demand, better pricing, easing cost pressure, stronger revisions, and constructive relative performance. When those elements begin to align, the sector is often telling the investor that the next phase of the cycle has already started, even if the latest reported quarter still appears mixed.

Chapter 6: Financial Statement Signals That Reveal Sector Strength or Weakness

The next layer of analysis is the statement level, where sector differences become visible not in abstract labels but in the way sales, costs, cash generation, and leverage show up on the financials. Two companies can appear similar on the surface and still tell very different stories once their statements are read against the economics of their sector. That is because reported figures are shaped by demand patterns, pricing power, asset intensity, working-capital needs, and financing habits that vary widely from one industry to another. In sectors such as banking, for example, financial soundness and balance-sheet structure are central to understanding strength or weakness, not peripheral details [45][24].

Revenue growth patterns across industries

Revenue growth rarely moves in a straight line across industries, and that unevenness is one of the clearest signals that sector analysis can provide. Some industries grow because demand rises steadily with population, income, or usage frequency. Others grow in bursts, driven by product cycles, pricing changes, regulation, or capacity additions. Still others may report headline growth that looks strong while the underlying business is merely recovering from a prior downturn. The analyst's job is not to ask whether revenue is rising, but why it is rising, how durable that growth is, and whether the pattern fits the economics of the industry.

In many industries, revenue growth is primarily a volume story. More units sold, more customers added, more transactions processed, or more assets managed usually point to genuine demand expansion. In other industries, revenue growth is more a function of price than volume. A commodity producer may show strong top-line growth simply because the market price of its product has increased, even if output is flat or falling. A software company may post rapid growth because it is adding subscribers and expanding usage, while a bank may grow revenue through loan balances, fee income, and spread changes. These different growth engines matter because they imply different levels of persistence. Volume-driven growth tied to structural adoption can last longer than growth driven by a temporary pricing spike.

Industry structure also shapes the shape of growth itself. In fragmented industries with low switching costs, revenue growth can be difficult to sustain because customers can move easily, competitors can undercut pricing, and market share gains are often temporary. In more concentrated industries, growth may be steadier because a few large players control distribution, capacity, or access to customers. Customer retention is especially important where relationships are sticky and the cost of switching is high. Research on retail banking, for example, has shown that retaining customers can improve revenue and reduce costs, underscoring how switching behavior affects growth durability in industries where loyalty and convenience matter [2].

Growth patterns also differ by maturity. Early-stage industries often show high percentage growth because the market is expanding from a small base, but that growth can be volatile and capital intensive. Mature industries typically grow more slowly, yet their revenue trends may be more predictable and less dependent on constant reinvention. A mature business does not need to post spectacular growth to be attractive; it may only need to outpace inflation, preserve share, and maintain pricing discipline. For the analyst, the key question is whether an industry's growth rate is naturally decelerating as it matures or whether it is being restrained by temporary conditions such as weak end demand, excess inventory, or aggressive competition.

Seasonality is another reason revenue growth patterns must be interpreted in context. Some industries are structurally seasonal because demand is tied to holidays, weather, school calendars, fiscal budgets, or crop cycles. A retailer may generate a disproportionate share of annual revenue in the fourth quarter; a construction-related business may see revenue cluster in warmer months; an agricultural supplier may be tied to planting and harvest schedules. In these cases, a single quarter's growth rate may be misleading unless it is compared with the same period in prior years and viewed alongside order patterns, backlog, or channel inventory. What matters is not whether revenue rose in one period, but whether the seasonal pattern is behaving normally or deviating from historical norms.

There is also a meaningful distinction between organic growth and growth produced by acquisitions, pricing, or accounting effects. Acquired revenue can make an industry look healthier than it is if consolidation is masking weak underlying demand. Price increases can lift reported growth even when transaction counts are flat. Currency translation can inflate or depress international revenue, creating the illusion of a change in demand that never actually occurred. Analysts therefore need to separate the components of reported growth whenever possible: unit growth, price growth, mix shift, acquisition contribution, and foreign exchange. That decomposition is especially important in industries where management teams are rewarded for top-line expansion and may emphasize the most favorable figure while leaving the slower-moving pieces in the background.

Revenue growth should also be judged alongside the industry's normal reinvestment needs. Some industries can produce strong growth with modest incremental capital, while others require heavy spending just to maintain the same pace. A business that grows revenue quickly but consumes large amounts of working capital, marketing expense, or capital expenditure may be creating a less efficient growth profile than a slower-growing peer with superior economics. This is why revenue growth cannot be read in isolation from margins, cash conversion, and balance-sheet strain. Two industries may report the same top-line rate and yet have completely different implications for earnings quality, because one converts growth into cash while the other merely converts cash into reported revenue.

The most useful comparison is often not between companies in different sectors, but between an industry's current growth pattern and its own history. If revenue growth is accelerating after a period of weakness, the analyst should ask whether the improvement reflects a genuine inflection in demand, a temporary restocking cycle, or an easy comparison base. If growth is slowing, the question becomes whether the slowdown is a normal late-cycle deceleration or the beginning of structural pressure from substitution, saturation, or competitive erosion.

Revenue growth patterns across industries are therefore less about ranking businesses by speed and more about identifying the economic forces that make growth repeatable, fragile, or misleading.

Margin analysis and operating leverage

Margin analysis is one of the clearest ways to see whether an industry is operating with structural strength or simply enjoying a temporary burst of demand. Gross margin shows how much pricing power a business has relative to its direct costs. Operating margin goes further by revealing how well the firm absorbs overhead, distribution expense, research spending, and other fixed costs. When these margins are read across a peer group, they can expose whether profitability is being driven by durable economics or by a short-lived combination of favorable volume, loose competition, or accounting timing. A company with expanding revenue but flat or declining margins may be growing in a way that is not economically efficient, while a company with stable revenue and rising margins may be benefiting from a stronger industry structure than the market recognizes.

For sector and industry analysis, the important question is not just how high margins are, but how they behave through the cycle. Some industries naturally carry high gross margins because their products are differentiated, their customers are sticky, or their intellectual property creates pricing leverage. Others operate on thin spreads because the business is highly commoditized, competition is intense, or customers can switch easily. The analyst should therefore compare margin levels only within a relevant peer set and then ask whether the current level is above, below, or near the group's historical range. A margin that looks mediocre in absolute terms may actually be excellent for a capital-intensive industry, while a margin that looks strong in isolation may be unsustainable if competitors are likely to undercut pricing.

Operating leverage adds another layer to that interpretation. It describes how changes in revenue flow through to operating profit when a company has a meaningful fixed-cost base. Businesses with high operating leverage often see profits rise faster than sales during an upswing because fixed expenses are spread over a larger revenue base. The reverse also happens: when demand slows, those same fixed costs can compress margins quickly. This is why sectors with heavy infrastructure, large labor commitments, or substantial technology and administrative overhead can produce dramatic earnings swings even when revenue changes look modest. In many cases, the market prices these businesses not on current earnings alone but on the implied sensitivity of future earnings to volume changes.

That sensitivity matters because operating leverage can be mistaken for operational excellence when it is really a function of scale and cost structure. A company may report a sharp increase in operating margin after a period of weak demand simply because revenue has recovered enough to absorb fixed costs that were already in place. The improvement is real, but it may not be repeatable at the same pace. Conversely, a business that is investing ahead of growth can show temporarily depressed margins even though the underlying economics are strengthening. The analyst has to distinguish between margin expansion caused by genuine efficiency gains and margin expansion caused by cyclical recovery, underinvestment, or temporary cost deferral.

Working-capital intensity often sits underneath these margin patterns. Industries with long inventory cycles, extended receivables, or large upfront production requirements can show earnings that look healthy while cash conversion remains weak. In those cases, margin analysis should be paired with an examination of how much revenue growth is being financed by balance-sheet expansion. Research on mining companies, for example, has found that working capital, leverage, asset turnover, and net profit margin all help explain earnings growth, underscoring that profitability and capital structure cannot be separated cleanly in capital-intensive sectors [72]. The same logic applies more broadly: a margin trend is more informative when it is viewed alongside the firm's funding needs and operating efficiency.

Industry structure also affects how much operating leverage a company can safely carry. In a stable, concentrated industry with disciplined competitors, a fixed-cost model may be an advantage because volume gains can translate into strong profit growth. In a fragmented or price-competitive industry, the same fixed-cost model can become a liability because firms may be forced to cut prices just as costs remain locked in place. This is why margin analysis should always ask whether the industry rewards scale or punishes it. A company with high fixed costs in a business where demand is volatile may look efficient during good times but fragile when conditions soften. The margin profile then becomes a measure of resilience, not just profitability.

Analysts should also separate margin quality from margin level. A margin can improve because of better mix, higher utilization, or genuine pricing power, but it can also improve because of one-time reductions in marketing, maintenance, hiring, or research. Those cost cuts may lift near-term earnings while weakening the competitive position later. Likewise, a margin decline may not be a sign of deterioration if the business is intentionally spending to protect share, expand capacity, or enter a new market. In sector analysis, the key is to ask whether margin changes are consistent with the industry's economics and the company's stage in the cycle. When they are, they help forecast earnings with greater confidence; when they are not, they often signal that the reported numbers are telling only part of the story.

In practice, margin analysis and operating leverage are most useful when they are treated as a comparison tool rather than a standalone verdict. The analyst should look at gross margin, operating margin, and the gap between them, then compare those figures with revenue growth, cost behavior, and peer results. A widening gap between sales growth and profit growth can indicate leverage working in either direction. A stable margin profile across different demand environments can suggest a business with pricing discipline and a more durable cost base. A volatile margin profile can point to cyclicality, weak competitive positioning, or a capital structure that amplifies operating risk. In sector and industry work, that pattern often reveals more than the headline earnings number itself.

Cash flow quality versus accounting earnings

Accounting earnings begin with accruals, and that is both their strength and their weakness. They are designed to match revenues and expenses to the period in which economic activity occurs, even when cash has not yet moved. In many industries, that produces a clearer picture of performance than cash flow alone. But the same flexibility that makes accrual accounting useful also creates room for distortion. Revenue can be recognized before collection, expenses can be deferred, reserves can be adjusted, and estimates can be revised in ways that make earnings look smoother than the underlying business really is. For sector analysis, the key question is not whether accrual accounting is legitimate—it is whether the earnings a company reports are being supported by real operating cash or by accounting choices that are unusually aggressive for that industry.

Cash flow quality is therefore not just a matter of how much cash a company generates, but how reliably that cash is produced and how closely it tracks reported profit. A business with high-quality cash flow converts sales into cash in a predictable way, with limited dependence on unusual working-capital swings, one-time gains, or accounting adjustments. In contrast, low-quality cash flow often appears when reported earnings rise faster than collections, when receivables build, when inventories accumulate, or when payables are stretched to create temporary relief. Those patterns may be acceptable in some sectors and alarming in others. A distributor with seasonal inventory builds may show a temporary cash outflow that is entirely normal, while a software company that reports strong earnings but weak collections may be signaling that its revenue quality is weaker than the headline suggests.

The distinction matters because sectors differ in the way they naturally convert earnings into cash. Asset-light subscription businesses, for example, may produce relatively stable operating cash flow because customers pay in advance or in recurring installments. Capital-intensive industries, by contrast, may report respectable accounting profits while consuming cash for equipment, maintenance, or expansion. That does not automatically make the earnings low quality; it means the analyst must separate growth investment from earnings inflation. In some sectors, cash flow will lag earnings during expansion because working capital is being deployed to support higher sales. In others, cash flow may temporarily exceed earnings because customers pay quickly and suppliers finance part of the business. The analyst's task is to determine whether the pattern is structural, cyclical, or a sign of accounting strain.

One of the most useful tests is whether earnings are being converted into cash at a pace consistent with the industry's normal operating model. Persistent gaps between net income and operating cash flow deserve attention, especially when the gap widens over multiple periods. If revenues are rising but receivables are rising faster, the company may be booking sales that are harder to collect. If margins improve while inventory also rises sharply, the business may be producing ahead of demand or relying on channel loading. If earnings are supported by repeated reserve releases, favorable estimates, or gains that do not recur in the ordinary course of business, the reported trend may be less durable than it appears. None of these signs proves manipulation on its own, but together they can indicate that accounting earnings are running ahead of economic reality.

Sector context is essential because the same accounting pattern can mean different things in different industries. In a bank or insurer, earnings quality is tied to loan loss assumptions, reserve adequacy, underwriting discipline, and the timing of claims or credit events. In a retailer, it may depend on inventory valuation, markdown policy, and the speed of cash collection from customers. In a manufacturer, it may hinge on utilization rates, warranty reserves, and the relationship between production and shipment timing. In each case, the analyst should ask whether the reported earnings are being supported by the sector's normal cash-generating rhythm or whether management is leaning on estimates that make the current period look better than the next one is likely to be.

Research on financial reporting quality shows that incentives and institutional setting matter because accounting numbers are not produced in a vacuum; they are shaped by the surrounding regulatory, legal, and governance environment [16]. That point is especially relevant in sector analysis because industries differ in how much discretion management has over estimates, timing, and classification. Where incentives to manage earnings are stronger, the gap between accounting profit and underlying cash generation becomes more important to inspect. The analyst does not need to assume bad faith. It is enough to recognize that reported earnings are a negotiated representation of performance, while cash flow is harder to dress up for long.

A disciplined reading of cash flow quality asks a few simple questions. Are operating cash flows keeping pace with earnings over time? Are working-capital changes consistent with the industry's normal cycle, or are they being used to inflate current results? Are capital expenditures supporting future growth, or are they masking the fact that maintenance needs are higher than management admits? Are nonrecurring items truly nonrecurring, or do they appear every year under a different label? When these questions are answered in the context of the sector, the analyst can distinguish businesses that are creating value from those that are merely reporting it.

Balance sheet risk and capital structure by sector

Balance sheet risk is not distributed evenly across sectors because the balance sheet itself is shaped by the economics of the business. Some industries naturally require heavy fixed assets, long-lived projects, or large working-capital commitments, while others can scale with relatively little permanent capital. That difference matters because leverage is not just a financing choice; it is often an operating feature of the industry. A utility, pipeline, airline, telecom, bank, or infrastructure business may carry more debt than a software or services firm because its assets and cash flows are built around large upfront spending and long recovery periods. In contrast, asset-light businesses can often support growth with less borrowing, which gives them more flexibility when conditions tighten.

For the analyst, the first question is not whether debt is "high" in the abstract, but whether the capital structure is appropriate for the sector's cash flow profile. A company with stable, regulated, or contract-based cash flows can usually sustain more leverage than one whose revenue is volatile or highly cyclical. The same debt-to-equity ratio can mean very different things depending on the predictability of earnings, the intensity of reinvestment, and the ease with which management can reduce costs in a downturn. In a capital-intensive sector, leverage may be part of the normal economic model; in a cyclical sector with thin margins, it can become a source of fragility very quickly.

This is why balance sheet analysis should be read alongside the sector's operating rhythm. Industries that require ongoing asset replacement or large project funding tend to accumulate debt because internal cash generation is often insufficient to fund both maintenance and expansion at the same time. Infrastructure businesses, for example, are often judged not only by profitability but by the cost of capital required to build and maintain the underlying network [75]. That makes interest-rate exposure especially important, because refinancing risk and higher borrowing costs can alter the economics of the entire sector even when reported earnings still look acceptable. In such cases, a seemingly manageable balance sheet can become strained if capital markets tighten or if regulators change the allowed return on invested capital.

Capital structure also reflects how much uncertainty a sector faces about future earnings. When cash flow is stable and visibility is high, debt can enhance returns without adding excessive risk. When earnings are more exposed to commodity prices, consumer spending, or competitive shocks, leverage amplifies downside as well as upside. This is particularly important in sectors where the business cycle and the financing cycle are closely linked. A company may look healthy at the peak of the cycle because strong profits make leverage appear modest, but that same leverage can become dangerous when margins compress and asset values fall. Analysts who focus only on peak-period ratios often miss this asymmetry.

Financial institutions deserve special attention because their balance sheets are not simply larger versions of industrial balance sheets; they are the core of the business model. For banks and similar lenders, leverage is intrinsic, and the real question becomes the quality of assets, the stability of funding, and the adequacy of capital under stress. The Irish banking crisis illustrated how quickly apparent strength can vanish when lending standards weaken, funding becomes fragile, and asset values deteriorate at the same time [38]. In sectors like banking, capital structure analysis must therefore include regulatory capital, deposit concentration, maturity mismatch, and exposure to correlated losses, not just headline leverage ratios.

The energy sector offers another useful example because its capital structure is shaped by both physical asset intensity and policy pressure. Energy companies often require large, long-duration investments, but they also face shifting expectations around transition risk, regulation, and future demand [51]. That combination can make balance sheets more vulnerable than they appear on a static basis. A firm may have ample asset coverage today, yet still face pressure if project returns weaken, financing costs rise, or capital markets demand a higher risk premium for long-lived assets. In such sectors, debt is not merely a measure of solvency; it is a claim on future strategic flexibility.

Working capital deserves the same sector-based treatment. Retailers, distributors, manufacturers, and agricultural businesses can all report very different balance sheet risk depending on inventory levels, receivables collection, and seasonal funding needs. A business with fast inventory turnover and quick customer payment may operate safely with moderate leverage, while another with long production cycles or slow collection can experience stress even with similar absolute debt. In agriculture, for example, productivity and capital use are tightly linked to resource constraints and operating conditions, which means liquidity management can be just as important as long-term leverage [1]. The point is that balance sheet risk is not only about the amount of debt outstanding; it is also about how quickly cash can be converted from operations when the environment turns less favorable.

A sector-aware capital structure analysis also asks whether the company has room to absorb shocks without sacrificing strategic options. Does it have maturities clustered in the next two years? Is a large share of debt floating-rate? Are covenants tight enough to constrain investment during a slowdown? Is management using debt to fund productive assets, or to support buybacks and distributions that may be hard to sustain later? These questions matter because sectors differ in how quickly they can recover from stress. A firm in a stable, regulated industry may be able to refinance and wait for conditions to improve, while a cyclical business with weak balance-sheet protection may be forced to dilute shareholders, cut investment, or sell assets at unfavorable prices.

Chapter 7: Valuation in Context —Comparing Companies the Right Way

Valuation only becomes useful when it is read against the economics of the business being valued. A multiple that looks ordinary in one industry may be stretched in another, not because investors are inconsistent, but because they are pricing different patterns of growth, risk, capital needs, and durability. The task, then, is not to force every company into the same valuation yardstick, but to understand which yardstick fits the setting and what the market is actually discounting. That requires moving beyond headline ratios and asking what the comparison is really measuring.

Why valuation multiples vary by sector

Valuation multiples vary by sector because a multiple is not a pure measure of cheapness; it is a shorthand for how the market prices growth, durability, risk, and capital intensity in a particular business model. A company with recurring revenue, high returns on invested capital, and limited need for heavy reinvestment can often support a higher earnings or sales multiple than a company whose profits are more cyclical, more capital-hungry, or more exposed to commodity swings. The market is not simply rewarding popularity. It is discounting the quality and persistence of future cash flows.

This is why cross-sector comparisons can be misleading when they rely on the same multiple without adjustment. A software platform and a steel producer may both trade at what looks like a "reasonable" earnings multiple, but the meaning of that number is very different in each case. In the software business, a higher multiple may reflect predictable subscription revenue, low incremental delivery cost, and the possibility that margins can expand as scale increases. In the steel business, a lower multiple may reflect volatile pricing, heavy fixed assets, and earnings that can swing sharply with global supply and demand. The multiple is not just a price tag; it is a compressed summary of the business model's economics.

Growth expectations are one of the main reasons multiples diverge by sector. Investors usually pay more for businesses that can compound revenue and earnings for long periods without requiring a proportional increase in capital. That is especially true when the growth is repeatable rather than dependent on a one-time event, a short product cycle, or a temporary surge in demand. In contrast, sectors with mature end markets or limited structural growth often trade at lower multiples because the market sees fewer opportunities for sustained expansion. Even when current earnings are strong, the multiple may remain restrained if investors believe that growth will normalize or reverse.

Risk is the second major driver. A sector with stable demand, visible cash flows, and strong pricing discipline generally deserves a different valuation framework than one exposed to sharp swings in commodity prices, funding conditions, regulation, or consumer confidence. The more uncertain the future stream of earnings, the more investors tend to demand a discount. That discount is not arbitrary; it compensates for the greater chance that reported profits will prove temporary, that margins will compress, or that balance sheet stress will emerge when conditions weaken. In industries where customer switching is easy, competition is intense, or product differentiation is limited, the market often assigns a lower multiple because future profits are harder to defend. Research on retail banking, for example, shows how customer switching behavior is shaped by competitive conditions and retention dynamics, which helps explain why durability matters so much in valuation [2].

Capital intensity also matters because it changes the relationship between accounting earnings and real economic returns. Two businesses can report the same earnings, but if one must continually reinvest in plants, equipment, inventory, or regulatory assets to maintain those earnings, its valuation should usually be lower than that of a business that can grow with lighter reinvestment. This is why sectors such as utilities, telecom, industrials, and transportation often trade differently from asset-light service or software businesses. The market is not just asking how much profit is reported today; it is asking how much of that profit can be converted into free cash flow after the business has paid to stay in place.

Sector-specific multiples also reflect the way investors think about the persistence of margins. In some industries, high margins are structurally supported by brand strength, network effects, switching costs, or regulatory protection. In others, high margins attract competition and tend to fade as supply responds. A multiple that appears expensive on current earnings may still be justified if the market believes margins are durable and reinvestment needs are modest. Conversely, a low multiple may not signal opportunity if earnings are elevated only because the industry is temporarily enjoying favorable conditions. The valuation question is never just "what is the multiple?" but "what does the multiple imply about the future shape of the business?"

There is also a difference between sectors that are valued on current earnings and sectors that are valued on normalized or forward earnings. In cyclical industries, current profits can be unusually high near the top of the cycle or unusually depressed near the bottom, so the headline multiple can mislead unless it is interpreted against normalized conditions. That is why analysts often compare valuation to through-cycle earnings, not just the latest reported number. In more stable sectors, by contrast, current earnings may be a better proxy for sustainable earnings power, which can make the same multiple more informative. The key is to match the valuation method to the earnings pattern of the industry, rather than forcing every business into the same template.

Sector differences in valuation are therefore not a market inefficiency to be corrected; they are often a rational expression of different economic realities. The analyst's task is to determine whether the market's implied assumptions are too pessimistic, too optimistic, or appropriately cautious relative to the sector's structure. That requires looking beyond the multiple itself and asking what kind of business is being priced: one with durable cash generation and limited reinvestment, or one whose earnings are more exposed to the cycle, competition, and capital demands. Only then does the number become interpretable.

Relative valuation versus intrinsic valuation

Relative valuation asks what the market is willing to pay for one business compared with another. Intrinsic valuation asks what the business is worth based on the cash it can generate over time, discounted back to today. In sector and industry analysis, those are not competing ideas so much as different answers to different questions. Relative valuation is useful when the main task is comparison: Is this company richer or cheaper than its peers? Is the industry trading above or below its own history? Intrinsic valuation is useful when the main task is estimation: What is the business worth if its future cash flows, reinvestment needs, and risk profile are modeled directly?

The distinction matters because sector context affects both methods, but in different ways. Relative valuation is highly sensitive to peer selection. A software platform may appear expensive against the broad market and still be ordinary relative to other recurring-revenue businesses with similar growth and retention characteristics. A bank may look cheap on a price-to-book basis and still be fully valued if its return on equity is weak and its asset quality is deteriorating. The analyst is not just comparing numbers; the analyst is comparing economic models. If the peer group is wrong, the relative multiple can mislead even when the arithmetic is correct.

Intrinsic valuation is less dependent on peer labels, but it is not free from sector assumptions. The discount rate, terminal growth rate, reinvestment rate, and margin trajectory all reflect industry realities. Capital-intensive sectors require more reinvestment to sustain growth. Cyclical sectors demand more caution around normalized earnings. Highly regulated or structurally stable industries may justify different long-run assumptions than businesses exposed to rapid technological change. In other words, intrinsic valuation is not an escape from sector analysis; it is sector analysis translated into a cash flow model.

Relative valuation is often the faster tool and therefore the one investors reach for first. It is especially useful when markets are repricing an entire group, when the goal is to identify outliers, or when the analyst needs a quick sense of whether expectations have become too optimistic or too pessimistic. But relative valuation can become circular if the whole peer group is mispriced in the same direction. Entire industries can trade at elevated or depressed multiples for long periods because investors are collectively adjusting for growth, risk, or capital intensity. A seemingly "cheap" stock can remain cheap if the industry's economics are structurally weak, while a "rich" stock can stay expensive if the market believes its competitive position is unusually durable.

Intrinsic valuation is better suited to questions of durability, but it can create a false sense of precision. A discounted cash flow model may produce a neat fair value estimate, yet the output is only as good as the assumptions behind it. Small changes in margin, terminal growth, or discount rate can move the answer materially. That sensitivity is especially important in sectors where earnings are volatile or where the business model is still evolving. In those cases, a model can become more of a disciplined framework for thinking than a reliable point estimate. The value of the exercise is not that it produces certainty, but that it forces the analyst to make explicit judgments about what must be true for the stock to be worth the current price.

For sector analysis, the strongest approach is usually to let the two methods check one another. Relative valuation can reveal how the market is currently ranking a business within its field; intrinsic valuation can test whether that ranking is justified by cash flow economics. If a company trades at a premium to peers, the analyst should ask whether the premium reflects superior growth, better margins, lower risk, or stronger reinvestment opportunities. If a company trades at a discount, the analyst should ask whether the discount reflects temporary cyclicality, accounting noise, or a genuine structural disadvantage. The point is not to choose one method and ignore the other, but to use each as a control on the other's blind spots.

This is where sector and industry context becomes especially powerful. Relative valuation is most informative when companies are truly comparable in customer behavior, capital structure, and margin logic. Intrinsic valuation is most informative when the analyst can reasonably forecast the economics of the business across a full cycle. When those conditions are not present, both methods require adjustment. A company with unusually high growth may deserve a premium multiple even before its cash flows are fully visible. A company in a declining or highly cyclical industry may need a normalized earnings base rather than a single-year figure. In both cases, the analyst is not abandoning valuation discipline; the analyst is adapting it to the terrain.

There is also a behavioral difference in how investors use the two frameworks. Relative valuation tends to anchor decisions to what others are paying now, which can be efficient but also crowd-driven. Intrinsic valuation tends to anchor decisions to an internal estimate of worth, which can be more independent but also more assumption-heavy. Sector analysis improves both by narrowing the range of reasonable comparisons and by clarifying which assumptions are economically defensible. When used together, relative and intrinsic valuation do not merely produce two numbers. They create a more reliable range within which an investor can judge whether a stock is attractively priced, fairly priced, or priced for conditions that are too optimistic or too cautious for the industry it inhabits.

Growth, risk, and capital intensity adjustments

Growth adjustments matter because valuation multiples are often a shorthand for how much expansion the market expects to continue. A business with rapid revenue growth can deserve a higher multiple than a slower-growing peer, but only if that growth is both durable and economically valuable. The analyst has to ask whether the growth is coming from share gains, market expansion, pricing, acquisitions, or a temporary rebound from an unusually weak base. Those sources are not equivalent. Organic growth supported by recurring demand and expanding unit economics usually deserves more credit than growth purchased through discounting, loose credit terms, or aggressive acquisition spending. In sector and industry work, the point is not to reward the fastest headline growth, but to separate growth that can compound from growth that merely fills a short window in the cycle.

That adjustment becomes especially important when comparing industries with very different starting points. A mature utility, for example, may grow slowly but still create substantial value if it earns stable returns on a large regulated base. A software platform may grow faster, but if retention weakens or customer acquisition costs rise faster than lifetime value, the growth may be less valuable than it first appears. In practice, slower growth can justify a richer valuation when it is paired with predictability, while faster growth may justify a lower valuation when it is uncertain, expensive to sustain, or vulnerable to competition. The analyst should therefore normalize growth for quality, not just rate, and should pay attention to whether growth is expanding or merely preserving the franchise.

Risk adjustments are equally important because the same earnings stream does not deserve the same multiple when its volatility, cyclicality, or downside exposure differs. Investors do not pay the same price for a dollar of earnings that is stable across the cycle and a dollar of earnings that can disappear in a downturn. Risk in sector analysis includes more than business volatility; it also includes customer concentration, regulatory exposure, commodity sensitivity, leverage, litigation, and the reliability of management's assumptions. A company may report impressive current results, but if those results depend on favorable macro conditions or unusually loose financing, the valuation should reflect the possibility that conditions reverse. The market often compresses multiples in industries where earnings are highly sensitive to external shocks because the path from reported profit to realized cash is less dependable.

Capital intensity creates another necessary adjustment because it affects how much of reported profit can actually be converted into free cash flow. A business that must continually reinvest in plants, equipment, networks, inventory, or working capital has less distributable cash than a business that can grow with relatively modest reinvestment. This is why two companies with similar accounting earnings can command very different valuations. The first may be consuming most of its operating profit just to maintain its asset base, while the second may be converting a large share of earnings into cash that can be reinvested, repurchased, or returned to shareholders. Capital intensity also influences resilience: when a downturn arrives, a company with heavy fixed obligations and ongoing reinvestment needs may see cash flow deteriorate much faster than reported earnings suggest.

These adjustments are not meant to produce a rigid formula, because valuation is still a judgment about expected future economics. But they do give the analyst a disciplined way to compare businesses that appear similar on the surface. A common error is to compare companies on a single multiple without asking whether one is growing faster because it is taking on more risk, whether one is less risky because it requires less reinvestment, or whether one's reported earnings are inflated by temporarily low capital spending. In industries where maintenance spending is understated, working capital is rising, or asset replacement is deferred, earnings can look richer than they are. In industries with low reinvestment needs and strong cash conversion, the opposite can be true: reported earnings may understate the economic value being created.

Sector and industry analysis becomes more precise when growth, risk, and capital intensity are treated as linked variables rather than separate checkboxes. High growth often comes with higher uncertainty, higher reinvestment demands, or a shorter period of competitive advantage. Lower growth often comes with greater visibility, but not always with lower risk if the business is burdened by leverage or structural decline. The analyst's task is to decide whether a company's valuation reflects the right mix of these factors relative to its peers and its own history. That means adjusting for the economic setting of the industry, not just the company's recent performance, and asking whether the market is pricing a durable compounding machine, a cyclical rebound, or a capital-hungry business whose earnings quality is thinner than the headline numbers imply.

Applied general equilibrium work in sector analysis has long emphasized that industries cannot be assessed in isolation because policy, resource allocation, and input constraints shift value across related parts of the economy [4]. The same logic applies to valuation: growth, risk, and capital intensity must be interpreted in context, because changes in one part of the business model often alter the others. A company that appears expensive on current earnings may simply be carrying the burden of heavy reinvestment today in exchange for stronger future cash generation. Another may look cheap because its growth is slowing and its risk profile is rising. The valuation task is to identify which of those stories is embedded in the numbers before a comparison is made.

Avoiding false comparisons between unrelated businesses

A false comparison begins when two businesses are placed side by side simply because they occupy the same broad market label or appear to share a similar financial statistic. Two companies may both be "growth stocks," both trade at 20 times earnings, or both report rising revenue, yet those similarities can conceal radically different economics. One may be a subscription business with recurring revenue, low capital needs, and high customer retention; the other may be a project-based operator with lumpy demand, heavy reinvestment, and volatile margins. Treating those companies as if they belong on the same valuation shelf leads to distorted conclusions about quality, durability, and risk.

The first safeguard is to compare businesses only after asking what actually drives their results. Revenue growth means something different in a company selling essential replenishment products than in one selling discretionary upgrades, and it means something different again in a business whose growth is fueled by acquisitions or temporary price increases. Margin structure also cannot be read as a universal scorecard. A 30 percent operating margin may be outstanding in one industry and ordinary in another, depending on gross margin structure, sales intensity, regulatory burden, and capital intensity. Without that context, investors risk mistaking a structurally advantaged model for a merely cyclical improvement, or a weak model for a temporary setback.

A second safeguard is to avoid using broad sector labels as if they were precise peer definitions. Sector membership is often too coarse to support direct comparison. A software platform, a semiconductor manufacturer, and a hardware distributor may all sit under a technology umbrella, but their earnings drivers are not interchangeable. The same problem appears in consumer-facing businesses, where one company may sell necessities with stable repeat demand while another depends on fashion, promotions, or economic confidence. The appropriate comparison set is usually smaller than the sector and sometimes narrower than the industry label suggests. The analyst has to identify whether the relevant economic drivers are pricing power, installed base, usage frequency, regulation, inventory turnover, or some other feature that truly links the businesses.

False comparisons are especially dangerous when investors compare valuation multiples without adjusting for business model differences. A lower price-to-earnings ratio does not automatically mean a stock is cheaper if its earnings are more cyclical, more leveraged, or less reliable. Likewise, a higher multiple does not automatically imply overvaluation if the company earns superior returns on capital and reinvests at attractive rates for a long period. The market often assigns different multiples to businesses because it is pricing different levels of visibility, reinvestment needs, and cash flow conversion. Comparing those multiples without asking why they differ can lead to superficial bargains and missed quality.

This is why earnings quality matters as much as earnings magnitude. Two firms can show the same earnings growth while one is converting those earnings into cash and the other is relying on stretched working capital, aggressive accruals, or temporary expense deferrals. Financial reporting quality itself is not uniform across environments; it is shaped by institutional and market conditions, and research has shown that reporting quality is closely tied to broader country attributes and accounting regimes [16]. Even within one market, however, industry structure still affects how much confidence an analyst should place in reported numbers. A business with stable billing, low returns, and short collection cycles deserves a different interpretation from one with long project timelines, large estimates, or complex revenue recognition.

The same caution applies to balance sheet comparisons. Leverage is not equally risky across all businesses, and debt cannot be judged apart from the cash flow pattern that supports it. A utility, a telecom operator, and a consumer brand may all carry debt, but the stability of their cash generation, the predictability of their capital spending, and the flexibility of their pricing power are not the same. Comparing leverage ratios without adjusting for these differences can create the illusion that one company is prudently financed and another is reckless, when the real distinction may be the structure of the industry itself. In some cases, a balance sheet that looks conservative on paper may still be fragile if cash flows are exposed to sharp swings in demand or input costs.

The analyst's task, then, is not to eliminate comparison but to make it more exact. That means comparing like with like: recurring revenue with recurring revenue, capital-intensive operators with capital-intensive peers, cyclical businesses with cyclical peers, and businesses exposed to similar pricing and demand conditions with one another. It also means resisting the temptation to rank companies by a single metric divorced from context. A good comparison isolates the driver that matters most and asks whether the market is rewarding or penalizing that driver appropriately. When the comparison set is wrong, the conclusion will usually be wrong too, even if the spreadsheet is technically correct.

Chapter 8: Building a Repeatable Sector Analysis Framework

Once the broader sector and industry context has been established, the analyst needs a consistent way to turn that context into judgment. A repeatable framework matters because sector analysis can otherwise become a collection of disconnected impressions: a strong quarter here, a weak margin there, a favorable macro headline, a troublesome valuation multiple. The goal is to impose order on that complexity without pretending that every industry behaves the same way. In practice, the best frameworks do not replace judgment; they discipline it. They help the investor ask the same core questions each time, compare companies on a like-for-like basis, and separate durable strength from temporary advantage.

A practical research checklist

A practical research checklist is useful only if it forces the analyst to move in the right order. The first question is always whether the company belongs in the right economic neighborhood. If the classification is wrong, every later comparison becomes less reliable. Confirm the sector, industry, and subindustry, then ask whether the firm's real earnings drivers match the label. A software company with recurring subscriptions should not be analyzed like a one-time license vendor; a lender exposed to consumer credit should not be treated like a fee-based financial platform. The point is not bureaucratic accuracy. It is to make sure the peer set reflects the forces that actually shape revenue, margins, and valuation.

Next, identify the dominant demand driver for the business. Ask what causes customers to buy, replace, renew, or delay purchases. Some industries are driven by household income, some by business investment, some by commodity prices, some by regulation, and some by technological adoption. A useful checklist asks whether demand is discretionary or essential, recurring or episodic, and elastic or resistant to price changes. It also asks whether demand is tied to new unit growth, replacement cycles, usage intensity, or a one-time project backlog. That distinction matters because the same reported growth rate can mean very different things depending on whether it reflects durable expansion or a temporary pull-forward.

Then examine the industry structure that governs profitability. Look for the number of meaningful competitors, the ease of entry, the strength of switching costs, the degree of product differentiation, and the presence of scale advantages or network effects. These factors determine whether good times are likely to persist or attract competition that erodes returns. In industries with weak barriers, strong margins can be temporary even when recent results look impressive. In industries with structural protection, modest growth can still support exceptional economics. Research on knowledge-based value creation has shown how intangible assets such as human capital and organizational capability can become major value drivers in modern firms [85], which is why a checklist should include not only visible assets but also the less obvious sources of competitive durability.

After structure comes the cycle. Determine where the industry sits relative to capacity, inventory, pricing, and capital spending. Ask whether the group is in expansion, stabilization, slowdown, or recovery. Check whether current earnings strength is being helped by favorable comparisons, low input costs, tight supply, or aggressive pricing. Then test whether those conditions are likely to persist. A business can look fundamentally strong while actually sitting near the top of its cycle, where margins are elevated and expectations are already stretched. The checklist should force the analyst to separate current performance from normalized performance, because valuation is usually anchored to what the market thinks can continue.

Financial statement review should be tailored to the sector rather than applied mechanically. Revenue quality, margin behavior, working-capital needs, and balance sheet risk all deserve attention, but the meaning of each item changes by industry. In a capital-light, recurring-revenue business, cash conversion and retention may matter more than physical asset turnover. In a capital-intensive business, depreciation, maintenance spending, and leverage deserve closer scrutiny. In industries with heavier reliance on people and expertise, human capital can be a critical operating asset even when it is not fully visible on the balance sheet [86]. The checklist should therefore ask not just whether the numbers are improving, but whether they are improving for reasons that are repeatable, funded, and consistent with the economics of the business.

Valuation should be checked only after the operating picture is understood. Compare the company with its true peers, not with an arbitrary market average. Ask whether the current multiple reflects superior growth, better margins, lower risk, or stronger capital efficiency—or whether it simply reflects investor enthusiasm. Then test the multiple against the industry's structural characteristics. A business with durable cash flow and limited reinvestment needs may deserve a premium, while a cyclical or capital-hungry business may deserve a discount even when the recent quarter looks strong. The checklist is not complete until the analyst can explain why the market is paying the current price and what would have to happen for that price to be justified.

A disciplined research process also requires a final layer of judgment: what could break the thesis. Identify the key risks that are specific to the sector and industry, not just the company. These may include regulatory changes, commodity swings, customer concentration, funding stress, labor shortages, technology displacement, or governance weaknesses. In infrastructure-heavy or essential-service industries, corruption, weak oversight, and execution problems can distort outcomes and impair value creation [89]. The purpose of this step is to avoid treating risk as a generic footnote. A good checklist asks which assumption matters most, how it could fail, how quickly the failure would show up in the numbers, and whether the balance sheet or competitive position can absorb the shock.

Used this way, the checklist becomes more than a research aid. It becomes a filter that keeps analysis connected to the real drivers of business performance. The analyst starts with classification, moves through demand and structure, checks the cycle, reads the statements in context, tests valuation against peers, and finishes by stress-testing the thesis. Each step narrows the range of plausible outcomes. That is the practical value of sector and industry analysis: not to produce certainty, but to make judgment more defensible, comparisons more meaningful, and decisions less vulnerable to the illusion that every company lives on its own island.

Screening for sector leaders and laggards

Screening is the point where sector analysis becomes operational. Rather than asking whether a company is interesting in the abstract, the analyst asks whether it is leading or lagging within its own economic neighborhood. That question matters because a stock can look strong on a standalone basis and still be underperforming the businesses that share its demand drivers, cost structure, and valuation logic. A sector leader is not simply a company with a high share price; it is a firm that is outperforming its peers on the measures that matter most for that industry, whether those measures are growth, margins, returns on capital, balance sheet resilience, or earnings consistency. A laggard is not always a weak business, but it is one whose results, expectations, or valuation are deteriorating relative to the group.

The first step is to screen on relative performance, not just absolute performance. Price charts can be useful, but they should be paired with fundamental comparisons. A company that has fallen less than its peers during a sector downturn may be showing resilience rather than weakness. Conversely, a stock that has risen sharply may still be a laggard if the entire industry has advanced more quickly. Relative strength in price often reflects relative strength in earnings expectations, but not always. That is why the screen should include both market-based and operating-based measures: revenue growth versus peers, margin trend versus peers, earnings revisions versus peers, and valuation versus peers. When those measures point in the same direction, the analyst has a cleaner signal.

A useful screen starts by separating structural leaders from cyclical beneficiaries. Structural leaders tend to hold up across different phases of the cycle because they possess durable advantages such as scale, pricing power, recurring demand, or superior execution. Cyclical beneficiaries may look like leaders during a favorable part of the cycle simply because the industry itself is improving. The distinction is important. A business that is winning only because its entire sector is in an upswing may not deserve the same confidence as one that continues to gain share, expand margins, and generate strong returns even as conditions normalize. Screening should therefore ask not only "who is doing well?" but "who is doing well for reasons that can last?"

The most informative leader-and-laggard screens usually combine several layers of evidence. Start with growth: compare recent revenue trends, order trends, or unit volumes against peers. Then move to profitability: gross margin, operating margin, and return on invested capital can reveal whether reported growth is being earned efficiently or purchased at a cost. Add cash flow quality, because some companies can show good earnings while consuming cash through working capital, heavy capital spending, or aggressive accounting. Finally, compare valuation. A firm that screens as a leader but trades at a severe discount may be signaling hidden risk, while a laggard trading at a premium may be priced for a turnaround that has not yet appeared. The point of the screen is not to pick one metric as decisive, but to identify alignment or conflict across metrics.

In practice, screening works best when the analyst uses peer-relative thresholds rather than universal cutoffs. A 10 percent revenue growth rate may be excellent in a mature utility-like industry and mediocre in a fast-growing software niche. Likewise, a 15 percent return on equity may be strong in one capital-intensive sector and ordinary in another. Sector analysis prevents the screen from becoming mechanically misleading. It also helps expose companies that are outperforming in the wrong way. For example, a business may show improving earnings per share because of share repurchases, even though operating performance is flat or deteriorating. Another may look weak on headline margins but be investing aggressively in a way that improves its competitive position. Screening is the beginning of judgment, not the substitute for it.

This is where earnings revisions become especially valuable. Analysts and investors often respond to what companies reported last quarter, but the market usually prices what it thinks will happen next. A sector leader often shows positive revisions to revenue, margins, or guidance before those improvements are obvious in the reported numbers. A laggard often shows the opposite: estimates drift lower even while management continues to emphasize temporary softness. Revisions are not always correct, but they are a powerful way to detect whether the market is changing its view of an industry's earnings power. When revisions improve across a group, the screen may be identifying an emerging leader before the broader market fully recognizes it.

The best screens also account for quality of leadership. Some companies lead because they have genuine competitive strength. Others lead because they have taken on more financial risk, cut costs unsustainably, or benefited from one-time conditions that will not repeat. That is why a sector leader should be tested against the durability of its advantage. If a company's leadership depends on unusually favorable commodity prices, unusually loose credit, or unusually aggressive promotional activity, the screen should treat that leadership cautiously. On the other hand, if a company is gaining share, preserving margins, and maintaining balance sheet flexibility while peers are under pressure, the leadership is more likely to be real. In that sense, the screen is not just sorting names into winners and losers; it is helping the analyst distinguish durable strength from temporary noise.

A final refinement is to look for leadership breadth. One strong company can be an exception. Several strong companies in the same subindustry suggest something deeper is happening at the industry level. When multiple firms in a group show better growth, better margins, and better revisions at the same time, the analyst is likely seeing a sector theme rather than an isolated story. That breadth can be especially useful for identifying laggards as well. If most peers are improving and one company is not, the underperformance may reflect company-specific weakness rather than sector pressure. Screening for leaders and laggards therefore serves two purposes at once: it highlights where capital may be flowing within the market map, and it helps separate company problems from industry conditions.

Creating a simple industry scorecard

A simple industry scorecard works best when it does not try to measure everything. Its purpose is to compress a large amount of sector and industry information into a small number of repeatable judgments that can be compared across companies and revisited over time. The analyst is not building a full valuation model at this stage. The goal is to create a disciplined snapshot of industry conditions so that later company analysis has a clearer frame of reference. A good scorecard makes it easier to see whether the industry environment is improving, deteriorating, or merely stable, and whether a company is benefiting from that environment or fighting against it.

The most useful scorecards focus on a handful of dimensions that capture the economics of the group. Demand trend is one of the first. Is end-market demand expanding, flat, or contracting? Pricing power is another. Can firms raise prices without losing volume, or are they forced into discounting to defend share? Competitive intensity matters as well. A fragmented industry with aggressive rivals usually produces thinner margins than a concentrated one with disciplined behavior. Capital intensity should also be included, because industries that require heavy reinvestment or frequent refinancing are more exposed to changes in credit conditions and return expectations. Finally, the scorecard should account for earnings quality, since reported growth is less meaningful if it is being driven by loose credit, working-capital release, or temporary inventory effects rather than durable operating improvement.

One practical way to build the scorecard is to use a simple 1-to-5 scale, where 1 signals weak conditions and 5 signals strong conditions. The analyst then assigns a rating to each factor based on available evidence, not intuition alone. For example, demand trend may be scored from order data, unit volumes, or management commentary. Pricing power may be inferred from gross margin behavior, promotional activity, or peer disclosures. Competitive intensity may be judged from market share stability, new entrants, and the frequency of industry price cuts. Capital intensity can be assessed through depreciation levels, maintenance spending, and balance sheet leverage. Earnings quality can be rated by comparing cash flow conversion, accrual behavior, and the consistency of reported results across the cycle. The exact labels matter less than the discipline of using the same method every time.

The scorecard becomes more useful when the analyst separates current conditions from structural characteristics. Current conditions describe what is happening now: whether demand is strengthening this quarter, whether inventory levels are normalizing, whether margins are under pressure, or whether financing is becoming tighter. Structural characteristics describe what tends to be true over time: whether the industry usually enjoys pricing power, whether it is capital intensive, whether customer switching costs are high, and whether competition tends to be rational or destructive. A weak quarter in a strong industry may be a temporary setback, while a strong quarter in a weak industry may be a cyclical bounce. The scorecard should preserve that distinction rather than blending everything into one impression.

To keep the scorecard from becoming subjective, it helps to anchor each rating to observable evidence. If demand is rated a 4, the analyst should be able to point to specific signs such as backlog improvement, rising shipment data, or positive revisions in guidance. If pricing power is rated a 2, there should be evidence of discounting, channel incentives, or margin compression despite steady volume. If capital intensity is rated a 5, the industry should clearly require substantial fixed assets, long payback periods, or persistent reinvestment. This approach does not eliminate judgment, but it makes judgment visible and testable. In practice, that is more valuable than a scorecard that appears precise but rests on vague impressions.

A useful scorecard also highlights where an industry sits in relation to its own history. A group can score well on current demand yet still be late in the cycle if margins are already elevated and competition is beginning to intensify. It can score poorly on near-term growth yet still be attractive if the industry is washing out excess capacity and setting up for a better phase later. This is one reason experienced analysts often treat the scorecard as a timing tool as much as a quality tool. It helps answer not only whether an industry is attractive, but whether the present setup is improving enough to justify closer attention or deteriorating enough to reduce exposure.

For example, a basic scorecard for a payment-processing or subscription software industry might show strong demand visibility, moderate to strong pricing power, moderate competitive intensity, low to moderate capital intensity, and generally high earnings quality. By contrast, a scorecard for an airline or commodity-linked industrial group may show highly variable demand, weaker pricing control, intense competition or cyclical overcapacity, heavy capital requirements, and more volatile earnings quality. Neither profile is automatically good or bad, but the scorecard makes the differences explicit. That clarity helps investors avoid comparing businesses as if they were governed by the same economics when they are not.

When used consistently, the scorecard becomes a bridge between broad sector analysis and company-specific judgment. It does not replace deeper research, but it gives that research a starting point. A company in a weak industry may deserve a lower baseline expectation even if its recent results look strong, while a company in a strong industry may deserve more patience when short-term noise distorts the numbers. The scorecard's value is that it forces the analyst to state the industry case in plain language before moving on to valuation, forecasting, or portfolio decisions. That discipline makes later comparisons sharper and reduces the chance of being swayed by isolated data points that do not reflect the industry's underlying economics.

Turning analysis into buy, hold, or avoid decisions

A buy, hold, or avoid decision is not a verdict on the company in isolation; it is a judgment about how the company's current position fits its industry setting, its competitive power, and the price investors are being asked to pay for that position. The same business can move from attractive to merely acceptable, or from acceptable to dangerous, without any dramatic change in the company itself. A richer valuation, a weakening industry backdrop, or a deterioration in peer performance can change the decision even when reported earnings still look solid. Sector and industry analysis gives the analyst a way to connect those moving parts instead of treating them as separate issues.

A buy decision is most defensible when several layers of evidence align. The company should be operating in an industry with favorable economics, or at least in a segment that is outperforming its broader group. Its earnings quality should look durable rather than inflated by temporary pricing, unsustainable cost cuts, or one-time demand surges. Its balance sheet should be capable of withstanding the normal volatility of the business, and its valuation should leave room for the expected risks. In practice, that often means the company is not only better than its peers, but better in a way that is likely to persist. Strong relative margins, stable customer retention, disciplined capital allocation, and a reasonable entry price together create the conditions for a buy.

A hold decision usually reflects a more balanced picture. The company may be fundamentally sound, but the industry may be mature, the cycle may be late, or the valuation may already discount much of the good news. In that case, the stock may still deserve a place in a portfolio, but not an aggressive one. Hold is often the correct answer when the business is high quality but fully valued, when the sector backdrop is neutral rather than supportive, or when the analyst lacks a convincing edge over the market's current expectations. It is also appropriate when the company is improving, but the improvement is still too early to justify a larger position. Holding is not indecision; it is recognition that the expected return does not yet justify a stronger commitment.

An avoid decision becomes appropriate when the industry structure is working against the company and the price does not compensate for that weakness. Poor industry economics can overwhelm company-level execution over time. If the field is characterized by low switching costs, intense rivalry, weak pricing power, or structurally high capital needs, then even a competent operator may struggle to produce attractive long-run returns. The same caution applies when the company's apparent strength is being supported by temporary conditions that are likely to reverse. A stock can be expensive not because investors are irrational, but because the market is still assuming a favorable environment that is already beginning to fade.

The decision process becomes more reliable when it asks three questions in order: What is the industry doing? How well is this company positioned within it? What is already reflected in the price? That sequence keeps the analyst from overreacting to isolated financial statements or headline growth rates. A company may report rising revenue, but if the industry is losing momentum, peers are cutting guidance, and margins are narrowing, the growth may not be sustainable enough to justify a buy. Conversely, a company with only modest reported growth may still deserve a buy if it is taking share in a favorable industry, generating strong cash flow, and trading at a discount to its own history and peer group.

Relative comparison is especially important because the market often rewards or punishes groups before individual results fully show up in the numbers. A company that appears average on an absolute basis may actually be one of the strongest names in a weak industry, while a company that looks impressive in isolation may simply be riding a favorable tide. Customer behavior can be a useful clue here. In banking, for example, longer retention tends to improve revenue stability and cost efficiency because the institution can spread acquisition costs over a longer relationship [2]. That kind of industry-level behavior helps explain why one bank may deserve a buy while another, with similar headline growth, may not. The analyst is not asking whether the company is merely growing; the question is whether the growth is occurring in a structure that supports durable value creation.

The final judgment should also reflect how much the market has already discounted the likely outcome. A strong company in a strong industry can still be a poor purchase if the stock price assumes perfection. A weaker company can sometimes be a hold, or even a speculative buy, if the valuation already reflects substantial damage and the downside is limited. But that requires a clear understanding of what would have to go right for the thesis to work. Sector and industry analysis improves this judgment by clarifying whether those expectations are realistic. It helps distinguish a business that is temporarily out of favor from one whose economics are structurally impaired, and it gives the investor a disciplined way to decide whether the evidence supports adding, maintaining, or avoiding the name.

Chapter 9: Applying Sector Analysis to Investment Strategies

Once a sector has been understood on its own terms, the next question is how that knowledge changes portfolio decisions. The answer is rarely mechanical, because sector analysis does not simply identify what is cheap or expensive; it clarifies where risk is concentrated, where return drivers are shared, and where timing matters more than usual. A sector can be attractive for one objective and unsuitable for another, depending on whether the investor is seeking capital appreciation, current income, or a more stable path through different market conditions. It also helps explain why two portfolios with similar holdings counts can behave very differently when they are exposed to the same economic shock.

Sector rotation and tactical allocation

Sector rotation is the practice of shifting exposure toward the parts of the market that are likely to benefit from the next phase of the economic and earnings cycle, while reducing exposure to groups that are more vulnerable to it. Tactical allocation is the portfolio expression of that idea. Instead of treating sector weights as fixed, the investor adjusts them in response to changing conditions in growth, inflation, rates, credit, and market leadership. The purpose is not to predict every move with precision, but to align capital with the environment that is most favorable to the businesses being owned.

This approach matters because sectors do not usually lead or lag for the same reasons. Some groups respond first to changes in liquidity and sentiment, while others respond later to changes in actual demand and profit growth. A rotation strategy tries to identify where the market is in that sequence. When the economy is improving and expectations are still cautious, cyclicals often gain attention because earnings can accelerate faster than the market expects. When growth is slowing and investors become more defensive, capital often moves toward businesses with steadier demand, stronger balance sheets, or more predictable cash flow. The logic is comparative: the question is not whether a sector is "good," but whether it is likely to be better or worse than alternatives over the chosen horizon.

Tactical allocation should be distinguished from speculation. Speculation often depends on a single forecast or a narrow event, such as a rate cut, a commodity move, or a policy announcement. Tactical sector allocation uses a broader framework. It combines macro signals, relative earnings revisions, valuation spreads, margin trends, and price leadership to decide whether a sector's risk-reward profile is improving or deteriorating. In that sense, it is a disciplined form of active management rather than a short-term market bet. The investor is still asking which businesses deserve capital, but the answer is filtered through the current stage of the cycle and the current behavior of the market itself.

One of the most useful inputs is relative earnings momentum. A sector can look expensive on trailing numbers and still be attractive if revisions are moving upward faster than the market has priced in. Likewise, a sector can look cheap and still be a poor tactical choice if estimates continue to fall and margins are under pressure. This is where the work of combining different valuation and fundamental perspectives becomes important. Research on valuation estimation has long shown that single methods can disagree, and that combining signals can improve decision quality in noisy markets [100]. In practice, sector rotation works best when valuation is paired with revision trends rather than used alone.

Price behavior also matters because markets often anticipate fundamental change before it appears in reported results. A sector that begins to outperform its benchmark after a long period of underperformance may be signaling that investors are discounting better conditions ahead. But price leadership should not be accepted uncritically. It has to be tested against the underlying fundamentals. If a group is rallying while earnings estimates continue to decline, the move may be driven more by positioning than by improving business conditions. Tactical allocation is strongest when price, revisions, and macro conditions point in the same direction.

Risk control is the part of the process that keeps rotation from becoming overreaction. Sector exposure can change quickly, but business fundamentals usually do not. A tactical shift should therefore be sized carefully, especially when the evidence is mixed. Broad sector benchmarks help here because they provide a neutral reference point for judging whether an overweight or underweight is actually meaningful.

Without a benchmark, an investor may believe a portfolio is diversified when it is simply drifting with recent performance. With a benchmark, the investor can see whether the portfolio is truly expressing a view or merely inheriting the market's latest preference [103].

For individual investors and advisors, the practical value of sector rotation is often in improving the timing of existing decisions rather than replacing long-term strategy. A retirement portfolio may still hold a strategic mix of sectors, but tactical tilts can reduce exposure to groups facing deteriorating earnings quality or increase exposure to groups where the cycle is turning favorable. For traders, the same framework can identify shorter-duration opportunities when leadership is changing quickly. For analysts, it provides a way to connect macro conditions to portfolio construction without losing sight of company-level discipline. In each case, the central discipline is the same: own the sectors whose earnings path, valuation setup, and market behavior best fit the current terrain.

Value opportunities within weak sectors

Weak sectors can still produce attractive investments, but only when the weakness is understood correctly. A sector may be out of favor because the market is discounting a temporary earnings slowdown, a cyclical trough, or a sentiment swing that has little to do with long-term asset quality. In those cases, the sector-level label can obscure value that is hiding in plain sight. The opportunity is not to buy weakness indiscriminately; it is to identify when the market has priced a group as if its problems are structural even though the underlying business economics remain intact.

The first task is to separate price weakness from fundamental weakness. A sector can trade poorly for months while its leading firms continue to generate acceptable margins, preserve balance sheet flexibility, and defend market share. That kind of underperformance often reflects a discounted outlook rather than a broken business model. By contrast, a sector may look cheap on headline multiples while its economics are deteriorating through excess capacity, margin compression, rising leverage, or persistent demand destruction. The presence of low valuation alone does not make a weak sector investable; it only signals that expectations have fallen. The analyst still has to ask whether expected returns are likely to recover faster than the market assumes.

One useful lens is the distinction between cyclical weakness and structural decay. Cyclical weakness usually appears when earnings are temporarily depressed by inventory correction, lower commodity prices, tighter credit, or a pause in end-market demand. In that setting, the sector may still possess durable franchises, but the current earnings base is too low to support market confidence. Structural decay is different. It appears when the industry's economics are being permanently altered by substitution, regulation, new technology, or a lasting change in buyer behavior. A weak sector can become a source of value only when the analyst can show that the market is treating a cyclical setback as if it were structural decline.

Within weak sectors, value often concentrates in the better-capitalized firms, the lowest-cost operators, and the businesses with the most resilient demand profiles. These companies can survive the downturn with less dilution, less refinancing risk, and less forced retrenchment than weaker peers. In other words, the sector may be weak, but not every participant is equally impaired. This is where sector analysis becomes especially useful for value investors: it helps distinguish the survivors from the casualties. The best opportunities are often found in firms that are temporarily punished because they belong to an unpopular group, even though they have stronger pricing discipline, better asset quality, or more conservative capital structures than the average company in the same industry.

Valuation discipline matters more in weak sectors than in strong ones because the risk of a value trap is higher. A low multiple may simply reflect the market's expectation that earnings are near a peak, margins are about to normalize lower, or capital requirements will rise. In such cases, the apparent discount is misleading because the denominator in the valuation ratio is not sustainable. The analyst should test whether normalized earnings, free cash flow, and return on invested capital remain credible under a more conservative operating assumption. If the answer is no, the stock may be cheap for a reason. If the answer is yes, the weak sector may be offering a mispriced entry point.

Sector weakness can also create opportunities when investor behavior becomes excessively uniform. Markets often sell entire groups together, even when the underlying businesses differ meaningfully in quality. That broad selling can push down valuations across a whole sector before the market has done the work of separating the high-quality operators from the weaker names. In those moments, relative analysis becomes especially important. The question is not whether the sector deserves a premium, but whether one company deserves a discount that is too severe relative to its peers. A business with stable cash generation, modest leverage, and a clear path through the downturn can become attractive simply because the market has applied the same pessimism to all names in the group.

There is also a timing element. Weak sectors often begin to offer value before the operating data looks obviously improved. That is because markets tend to discount recovery in advance of reported earnings. The earliest signs are usually not dramatic: slower deterioration in margins, stabilization in order trends, easing inventory pressure, better credit conditions, or reduced estimates of downside risk. For the patient investor, these signals matter because they suggest that the market's worst-case assumptions may already be embedded in the price. The goal is not to buy every struggling sector at the first sign of cheapness, but to recognize when the sector's earnings trajectory is likely to turn less negative before sentiment does.

In practice, the best value opportunities within weak sectors are usually found where three conditions overlap: the sector is unpopular, the company's competitive position is stronger than the market implies, and the financial structure can withstand the downturn long enough for the cycle or sentiment to improve. That combination is more important than any single ratio or headline metric. Weak sectors can be fertile hunting grounds, but only for investors who are willing to distinguish between temporary dislocation and permanent impairment, and who understand that the cheapest stock in a troubled group is often not the best value unless its business can endure long enough to benefit from the eventual re-rating.

Dividend and income considerations by industry

Dividend policy varies by industry because the cash generation profile of each business model varies. Some industries produce steady, repeatable cash flows and can support regular distributions without starving the business of needed reinvestment. Others require heavy spending just to maintain competitive position, so a high payout ratio may look attractive in the short run while quietly weakening long-term franchise strength. The analyst's task is not to ask whether a yield is high, but whether the industry's economics make that yield sustainable through a full cycle.

Utilities, pipelines, telecom networks, and certain real estate businesses are often associated with income because they tend to operate with relatively predictable demand and tangible assets that can be financed in part with debt. In these industries, dividends are often part of the investment case, not an afterthought. But even here, the quality of the income depends on regulatory stability, capital spending requirements, and access to financing. A utility with a stable rate base may support a dependable payout, while a capital-intensive network facing rising borrowing costs or mandated upgrades may see its dividend coverage narrow even if reported earnings appear intact. In other words, income strength is tied not just to current profits, but to the amount of cash left after sustaining the asset base.

Other industries are structurally less suited to generous payouts because they need to retain more capital to grow or to survive volatile conditions. Banks, for example, distribute income, but their payout capacity is constrained by capital adequacy, credit quality, and regulatory expectations. During periods of stress, dividend policy can change quickly because preserving capital becomes more important than maintaining a headline yield. Energy companies can also appear income-friendly, yet their distributions are often exposed to commodity cycles, reserve replacement needs, and project spending. In such cases, the dividend may be real, but it is not necessarily stable in the way investors often assume when they screen for yield alone. Research on distress in tourism and hospitality similarly highlights how financial strain can emerge quickly when demand weakens and balance-sheet resilience is limited [8].

For income investors, the critical question is whether the dividend is funded by recurring free cash flow or by temporary conditions that may not persist. A company can pay a large dividend while borrowing, selling assets, or underinvesting in maintenance, but those are not durable sources of income. Industry context helps reveal when a payout is being supported by stable economics and when it is being propped up by favorable timing. This is especially important in sectors where reported earnings can overstate distributable cash because of working-capital swings, deferred spending, or accounting treatments that do not immediately show the strain on liquidity.

Yield also has to be judged against the industry's normal capital intensity. A mature consumer-staples company may not need much reinvestment to keep its business healthy, so a moderate payout ratio can be appropriate. By contrast, an industrial manufacturer, software platform, or healthcare innovator may need to retain more cash to fund product development, equipment refreshes, regulatory compliance, or acquisitions. In those industries, a lower yield is not automatically a weakness; it may be the price of preserving future earnings power. Investors who ignore this distinction often confuse a restrained dividend policy with poor shareholder returns, when in fact retained earnings may be compounding value more effectively than cash distributions.

Industry structure also affects the reliability of dividend growth. Businesses with recurring demand, pricing discipline, and low disruption risk can often raise payouts gradually over time, which is often more valuable to long-term income investors than a static high yield. By contrast, industries exposed to rapid technological change, commodity volatility, or aggressive competition may offer high current yields that fluctuate with the cycle rather than with stable economic strength. A dividend that rises in good years and is cut in bad years can still be useful, but it should be treated as cyclical income, not bond-like income. That distinction matters for portfolio construction, retirement planning, and any strategy that depends on cash flow stability.

Financial professionals often evaluate dividend sustainability through coverage ratios, free cash flow conversion, leverage, and the consistency of capital spending relative to depreciation and maintenance needs. Those measures become more meaningful when compared within the same industry, because payout norms differ widely across sectors. The same 60 percent payout ratio can be conservative in one industry and aggressive in another. The same dividend yield can signal opportunity in a stable, well-covered business or distress in a company whose market price has fallen because investors expect a cut. Sector and industry analysis gives those numbers their proper frame, allowing the investor to distinguish durable income from income that is merely visible today.

Using sector analysis in diversified portfolio design

Sector analysis becomes especially useful in portfolio design when the objective is not to find the single best idea, but to assemble a set of holdings whose risks do not all respond to the same economic force. Diversification is often described as owning many securities, but that is only part of the story. A portfolio of twenty stocks can still be highly concentrated if those stocks all depend on the same demand driver, the same funding environment, or the same commodity price. Sector analysis helps reveal those hidden linkages. It shows when a portfolio is diversified by name but not by exposure, and when a collection of apparently different businesses is actually tied together by one macro outcome.

The first step is to identify the economic sensitivities that sit underneath the labels. A company may be classified as a consumer discretionary name, but its real behavior may be closer to a credit-sensitive cyclical if sales rise and fall with financing conditions. Another may sit in industrials, yet function like a quasi-defensive service provider because demand is tied to long-term maintenance contracts rather than new capital spending. Once those distinctions are clear, the portfolio can be designed around return drivers instead of ticker symbols. That means thinking in terms of growth sensitivity, rate sensitivity, inflation pass-through, commodity exposure, and balance sheet vulnerability, then deciding how much of each exposure the portfolio should contain.

Within that framework, sector weights become a risk-control tool as much as a return decision. A portfolio that is overweight banks, brokers, and insurers may look diversified across multiple companies, but it is still exposed to the same credit cycle, the same yield curve, and often the same regulatory climate. Likewise, a portfolio with heavy exposure to utilities, telecom, and REITs may appear balanced because the businesses differ operationally, yet all three can be sensitive to interest rates and yield-seeking investor behavior. Sector analysis makes these shared sensitivities visible before they become portfolio-level disappointments. It also helps an investor decide whether a concentration is intentional compensation for a known risk or an accidental buildup of correlated exposure.

That distinction matters because diversification is not only about reducing volatility. It is also about preserving flexibility across regimes. In one environment, cyclicals may lead because growth is improving and credit is available. In another, defensives may outperform because earnings quality and cash stability matter more than expansion. A portfolio designed with sector analysis can be built to participate in more than one regime without relying on a single forecast. The investor may still express a view, but the view is implemented as a tilt rather than an all-or-nothing bet. This is especially valuable for long-term capital, where the cost of being wrong about timing can be larger than the benefit of being right for a few quarters.

Sector analysis also improves the way investors combine core holdings and satellite positions. Core holdings are usually chosen for durability, liquidity, and broad participation in market returns. Satellite positions are where conviction is concentrated, often in areas where the analyst sees stronger earnings momentum, valuation dislocation, or cycle-specific opportunity. Without sector context, satellites can unintentionally duplicate the risk already present in the core. With sector context, the portfolio can be arranged so that the core provides stability while satellites introduce targeted upside from distinct economic drivers. That structure is useful for individual investors who want to express active views without letting those views dominate the entire portfolio.

For retirement portfolios and income-focused accounts, the same logic applies, but the emphasis shifts toward cash flow reliability and drawdown control. A high yield is not enough if the income stream depends on one fragile sector condition, such as cheap financing, stable commodity prices, or sustained consumer spending. Sector analysis helps distinguish between income that is supported by durable business economics and income that is merely being paid out during a favorable phase of the cycle. It also helps balance sources of income so that a single shock does not impair multiple holdings at once. An investor who owns several high-yield names across different sectors may still be under-diversified if those names all weaken when rates rise or credit tightens.

Professional portfolio construction often uses sector analysis to manage correlation before it shows up in a risk report. That is because correlations are not fixed; they tend to rise when markets become stressed and investors reduce exposure to the same kinds of risk simultaneously. A portfolio built with sector awareness can reduce that problem by mixing businesses whose earnings respond to different conditions. Some holdings may benefit from growth in economic activity, others from pricing power, others from defensive demand, and others from long-duration secular trends. Research on leading sector identification has also shown that working at the sector level can improve portfolio analysis by organizing market behavior into a more usable structure [104].

Used this way, sector analysis does not replace security selection; it gives security selection a portfolio context. A strong stock can still be a poor addition if it increases the portfolio's dependence on a single macro outcome. A mediocre stock can sometimes serve a useful role if it adds exposure the portfolio lacks and behaves differently from the rest of the holdings. The point is not to own every sector equally, but to make sector concentration deliberate, measured, and consistent with the investor's objectives. When portfolio design begins with that discipline, diversification becomes more than a count of positions. It becomes a map of how the portfolio is likely to behave when the market's terrain changes.

Chapter 10: Real-World Case Studies and Common Pitfalls

At this point, the analysis moves from framework to evidence, because the most revealing lessons in sector work often come from situations where the market's first interpretation is incomplete or simply wrong. Case studies are useful not because they supply neat templates, but because they show how the same earnings report can be read very differently once industry conditions, competitive behavior, and capital structure are taken into account. They also expose where investors tend to overreact, underreact, or draw conclusions from too little context. The examples that follow are meant to sharpen judgment by showing how sector dynamics shape the meaning of results, why some surprises are less surprising than they appear, and how a disciplined analyst separates a temporary disturbance from a deeper change in business economics.

Case studies across multiple sectors

Consider agriculture, where a company's results can look impressive or disappointing for reasons that have less to do with management skill than with water availability, input costs, crop pricing, and the practical limits of productivity. In that setting, revenue growth is often inseparable from yield conditions and resource efficiency. Research on water productivity in agriculture shows how closely output depends on the efficient use of constrained inputs [1]. For an investor analyzing an agribusiness, seed developer, fertilizer producer, or food processor, the key question is not simply whether reported sales rose, but whether the sector is benefiting from a favorable commodity environment, a temporary supply shortfall, or a durable improvement in productivity. A fertilizer company can post strong margins when crop prices are high and farmers are willing to spend, yet those same margins may prove fragile if acreage shifts, weather normalizes, or input affordability weakens. In other words, the sector context determines whether a good quarter reflects structural strength or just a cyclical tailwind.

Healthcare offers a different kind of lesson because the industry can combine secular demand growth with policy and capacity constraints. A hospital operator, device maker, or surgical-services provider may report steady demand even in a slowing economy, but that stability does not mean all earnings are equally reliable. Staffing shortages, reimbursement pressure, regulatory changes, and procedure mix can all change the quality of growth. The Global Surgery 2030 literature emphasizes the economic importance of access to surgical care and the scale of unmet need [3], which helps explain why demand can remain strong over long periods. Yet investors still have to separate volume growth from margin durability. A provider may benefit from more procedures, but if labor costs rise faster than reimbursement or if case complexity shifts unfavorably, earnings quality can weaken even while headline demand looks healthy. Here, the sector lens helps identify whether growth is being converted into cash or absorbed by operating friction.

Financials, especially retail banking, show how customer behavior can reshape earnings faster than many investors expect. In a bank, the reported numbers may appear stable until deposit costs, loan pricing, or customer retention begin to shift. Research on switching behavior in Chinese retail banking highlights how competition and customer mobility affect a bank's ability to retain business and preserve revenue [2]. That insight generalizes well: a bank with apparently modest churn can still be vulnerable if customers are highly rate-sensitive or if competitors offer better digital service, lower fees, or more attractive yields. The result is that net interest margin and fee income can erode before the deterioration is obvious in the headline earnings release. For an analyst, the important task is to ask whether the bank's profitability reflects a durable franchise or a temporary spread advantage that can disappear as soon as funding costs rise or competitors become more aggressive.

Retail provides a useful contrast because its earnings can be distorted by consumer sentiment, inventory discipline, and promotional intensity. A retailer may report a strong same-store sales figure, but that number can be driven by heavy discounting rather than genuine pricing power. Inventory management often matters as much as demand itself: too much stock leads to markdowns, while too little stock can suppress sales and frustrate customers. In this sector, one quarter of good earnings can be misleading if it is achieved by sacrificing future margin or by borrowing demand from the next period. The analyst has to compare the company not only with its own history but with the behavior of peers facing the same shopper, the same supply chain, and the same promotional environment. A retailer that consistently protects gross margin while maintaining traffic is telling a very different story from one that is merely clearing shelves.

Technology case studies often center on the difference between growth and monetization. A software company can produce rapid revenue expansion while still failing to generate proportional cash flow if customer acquisition costs are rising, renewals are weak, or product development spending is outpacing operating leverage. The market sometimes rewards top-line acceleration even when the business model has not yet proven its ability to convert scale into durable economics. That is why sector and subindustry context matter so much: recurring subscription software, semiconductors, hardware, and platform businesses may all sit under a broad technology label, but their earnings drivers are not interchangeable. A chip designer with strong intellectual property may deserve a very different valuation and risk assessment than a hardware assembler exposed to inventory cycles and price compression. The lesson is not that technology is inherently better or worse, but that the source of growth determines whether earnings are likely to persist.

Energy shows how quickly sector conditions can overwhelm company-specific narratives. When commodity prices move, they can lift or depress reported earnings across the group with little warning. A producer may appear to have extraordinary operating performance when in fact the improvement is mostly the result of pricing rather than efficiency. Conversely, a well-run company can look weak during a downturn because realized prices have fallen faster than costs can be adjusted. This is why investors often misread energy earnings surprises: they treat them as proof of management execution when they may simply reflect the latest move in the underlying commodity. The sector lens forces a more disciplined reading. It asks whether the company is controlling costs, replacing reserves efficiently, and managing capital allocation well enough to survive the cycle, rather than assuming that a single profitable year proves long-term advantage.

Across these sectors, the pattern is the same even though the numbers look different. The market frequently overweights the latest earnings report and underweights the industry mechanics that produced it. A strong quarter in agriculture may reflect weather and crop economics; in healthcare, reimbursement and labor; in banking, customer retention and funding costs; in retail, inventory and promotion; in technology, monetization and reinvestment; in energy, commodity prices. Sector analysis does not remove the need to study the company. It makes that study more accurate by identifying which parts of the story belong to the business and which belong to the terrain beneath it. That distinction is what keeps investors from confusing a favorable environment with a durable edge.

How earnings surprises often reflect industry dynamics

Earnings surprises often look like company-specific events, but many of them are better understood as expressions of industry structure, timing, and competitive behavior. A surprise is not always the result of a management team suddenly becoming brilliant or careless. It may reflect a shift in pricing discipline across the peer group, a change in inventory positioning, a wave of customer demand that hits the whole industry at once, or a cost shock that affects all participants simultaneously. In that sense, the surprise is often less a verdict on the firm than a signal that the industry's earnings engine is running hotter or colder than the market expected.

This is especially important because analysts and investors tend to anchor on the headline number: revenue beat, margin miss, guidance raised, guidance cut. But the meaning of that headline depends on whether the industry is moving as a group. A revenue beat in a fragmented industry may indicate share gains, superior execution, or a temporary demand spike. The same beat in a concentrated industry may simply reflect a broad pricing cycle, a restocking wave, or a favorable mix shift that lifted the whole peer set. Likewise, a margin miss may appear to be a failure of cost control when it is actually the result of an industry-wide input-cost surge or a price war that no single firm can avoid.

One of the clearest ways industry dynamics show up in earnings surprises is through pricing behavior. In industries where supply is tight and demand is firm, companies often report upside surprises because realized prices move faster than consensus models. In industries where capacity is expanding or demand is weakening, the opposite happens: reported results disappoint because prices compress before analysts fully adjust their assumptions. The company may not have changed at all, but the market has misjudged the speed at which the industry pricing backdrop is shifting. This is why earnings season often becomes a referendum on whether the industry is in a period of discipline or a period of excess.

Inventory cycles are another common source of surprise. When customers or distributors build inventory aggressively, suppliers can post strong near-term revenue and earnings that later prove difficult to sustain. When inventories are drawn down, the reverse occurs: orders slow sharply even if end demand is not collapsing. These movements are easy to misread if the analyst focuses only on reported sales and ignores the position of the industry in the inventory chain. A company can beat estimates because the channel is restocking, then miss the next quarter because the same channel is working off excess stock. The surprise is real, but the cause is structural and cyclical rather than idiosyncratic.

Guidance surprises often reveal the same pattern. Management teams usually have better visibility into their own order books than outside analysts do, but they do not control the broader industry environment. If several competitors are seeing the same demand acceleration, a cautious company may raise guidance later than the market expects, even though the underlying industry is improving. If one firm cuts guidance while peers hold steady, the issue may be execution-specific. If multiple firms cut at once, the more likely explanation is that the industry itself has entered a weaker phase. The analyst should always ask whether the surprise is isolated or synchronized. Synchronization is often the clue that the driver is industry-wide.

This is where peer comparison becomes indispensable. A company that beats estimates by a modest amount while its peers beat by much more is not necessarily a leader; it may be lagging in an improving industry. Conversely, a company that misses while peers also disappoint may not be losing competitive footing at all. It may simply be exposed to the same demand or cost pressure as everyone else. Research on earnings surprises has also shown that investors can reward firms that appear atypical relative to peers, because the market often interprets deviation as a signal of distinctiveness rather than merely difference [106]. That makes it even more important to separate a true competitive advantage from an industry-wide anomaly.

The quality of the surprise matters as much as its direction. A beat driven by temporary price spikes, one-time cost deferrals, or aggressive channel loading carries less informational value than a beat driven by sustained demand, better mix, or durable share gains. A miss caused by deliberate investment in capacity, technology, or distribution may be less troubling than a miss caused by loss of pricing power or deteriorating end demand. In other words, the surprise itself is only the surface event. The analyst's task is to determine whether the industry backdrop is amplifying a temporary effect or revealing a deeper change in the earnings trajectory.

For that reason, earnings season should be treated as a testing ground for industry hypotheses. If companies across a sector are beating on revenue but missing on margins, the likely explanation is not a string of unrelated mistakes. It may be that pricing is holding up while costs are rising faster than expected. If the entire group is raising guidance, the industry may be entering a stronger demand phase or benefiting from a common supply constraint. If only one firm is standing out, the analyst should ask whether it has a genuine edge or whether the market is overreacting to a noise event. Earnings surprises are most useful when they are read as signals from the industry map, not as isolated flashes from a single quarterly report.

Mistaking temporary noise for structural change

Temporary noise becomes dangerous when it is mistaken for a change in the industry's underlying structure. A weak quarter, a sudden margin dip, or a one-time demand spike can look like evidence that a business has entered a new regime, when in fact the more important drivers have not changed at all. The analyst has to distinguish between fluctuations that arise from timing, weather, inventory movement, customer ordering patterns, promotions, or transitory cost shocks and shifts that alter the economics of the industry itself. That distinction matters because the market often reacts first to the visible number and only later to the cause behind it.

The easiest errors occur when a short-lived disruption is given too much explanatory power. A supplier outage may temporarily reduce revenue, but if customers simply deferred orders and later return, the event is noise. A retailer may show a margin decline because it cleared seasonal inventory at a discount, yet that does not necessarily mean the brand has lost pricing power. Likewise, a strong earnings beat can be misleading if it comes from channel fill, delayed expenses, or a brief lull in input costs. In each case, the result is real, but the interpretation may be wrong if the analyst assumes the latest quarter reveals a permanent shift in competitive position.

Structural change is different because it alters the rules under which the business operates. It shows up in more persistent ways: a sustained change in demand behavior, a new cost curve, a regulatory adjustment, a technological substitution, a permanent shift in customer preferences, or a change in capital intensity that affects returns across the whole peer group. If a sector's pricing power weakens because customers now have easier substitutes, that is structural. If margins compress because a one-time freight spike raises costs for one period, that is not. The challenge is that both can appear similar in the reported numbers if the analyst looks only at the headline variance instead of the pattern behind it.

A disciplined approach starts with asking whether the change is broad or isolated. If the same pressure is visible across several companies in the same industry, the odds rise that the move reflects a sector-level development rather than a company-specific mistake. If the issue shows up across multiple periods, not just one quarter, the case for structural significance strengthens further. The analyst should also look at whether management is describing the problem as temporary or whether the evidence points to a more durable shift in behavior. A single explanation from management is not enough, but it can help frame what to test against the data. In banking, for example, sector soundness is often assessed through quantitative signals that separate transient stress from deeper weakness, because reported results can mask whether a problem is cyclical or systemic [24].

Comparisons with prior cycles are especially useful, but only when they are used carefully. Investors often remember the last time a sector faced a similar headline and assume the current episode will resolve the same way. That can be useful when the underlying driver truly is recurring, such as inventory corrections or commodity price swings. It becomes dangerous when a new structural feature is present, such as a changed competitive landscape, a different funding environment, or a new technology that alters demand elasticity. The question is not whether history repeats exactly; it is whether the current disturbance belongs to a familiar pattern or marks the beginning of a different one.

The market itself can amplify the confusion. When a stock sells off sharply after a disappointing report, the price action may encourage investors to infer a deeper problem than the evidence supports. When a stock rallies on a strong beat, the same crowd may conclude that the business has turned a corner permanently. Yet price moves often reflect positioning, expectations, and sentiment as much as fundamentals. A sector that had been heavily discounted can produce an outsized reaction to a modest improvement, while a favored group can be punished for a minor miss. The analyst's task is to separate the market's emotional response from the business's actual condition.

This is why the most useful question is often not "Was the quarter good or bad?" but "What changed in the operating environment, and how likely is that change to persist?" If the answer involves a temporary mismatch between supply and demand, a delayed purchase cycle, or a short-term cost anomaly, the event may deserve attention but not a new thesis. If the answer involves a persistent shift in customer behavior, a new competitive entrant, or a cost structure that no longer supports prior margins, then the analyst should treat the event as evidence of structural change. The difference between those two readings is often the difference between patient analysis and costly overreaction.

Behavioral traps and analytical blind spots

Behavioral traps in sector analysis usually begin with a simple form of overconfidence: the belief that a familiar company story is the same thing as an accurate industry story. Investors often anchor on the most recent quarter, the strongest brand, or the most visible management narrative and then assume those signals are representative of the whole competitive field. That shortcut can be costly because sectors and industries do not move in lockstep with the headlines attached to individual names. A business can be executing well while its industry is losing pricing power, or it can be struggling temporarily inside a structurally strong group. The trap is not just missing information; it is misweighting the information that matters most.

Confirmation bias is especially dangerous in sector work because market participants tend to seek evidence that supports an existing view about a group. If an investor already believes a sector is "broken," every weak data point becomes proof of decline, while signs of stabilization are dismissed as noise. If the investor is bullish, the opposite happens: favorable commentary, a single earnings beat, or one improving indicator is treated as confirmation that the entire industry is turning. In both cases, the analyst stops testing the thesis against the full set of competitive and financial evidence. Good sector analysis requires the discipline to ask what would disprove the current view, not just what would support it.

Recency bias creates another blind spot by giving too much authority to the latest quarter, the last macro print, or the most recent price move. Sectors are cyclical, and industries often experience delayed effects from changes in rates, inventories, consumer demand, or capital spending. A strong month of order growth may reflect timing rather than trend; a weak quarter may reflect a temporary pullback rather than structural deterioration. When investors overreact to the newest data point, they often mistake the phase of the cycle for the direction of the business model. That leads to chasing strength near local peaks and abandoning solid businesses near local troughs.

There is also a subtle but important trap in treating industry averages as if they were neutral truth. Peer comparisons are useful, but they can hide dispersion inside the group. Averages can be distorted by one large incumbent, one distressed outlier, or one unusually profitable niche operator. That matters because the "typical" company in a sector may not be very typical at all. If the analyst relies too heavily on median margins, average valuation multiples, or broad index performance, the result can be a false sense of normalcy. The better question is whether the company sits near the center of the distribution, at the edge of it, or outside the range that defines the industry's real economics.

Another common blind spot is narrative inertia. Once a sector becomes associated with a dominant story—disruption, secular growth, commodity inflation, regulation, or collapse—that story can outlive the evidence that originally supported it. Investors may continue to price businesses as if the old regime still governs outcomes, even after cost structures, customer behavior, or competitive intensity have changed. The reverse also happens: a group that has disappointed for several periods may remain neglected long after the conditions that caused the disappointment have eased. In both cases, the market can become attached to a prior identity for the sector and ignore the slower-moving reality underneath.

Analytical blind spots also appear when investors confuse company quality with stock performance. A stock that has fallen sharply is not automatically a better value, and a stock that has risen sharply is not automatically overextended. Sector analysis is meant to separate operating reality from market emotion. That distinction becomes especially important when the broader market is rewarding momentum or punishing anything associated with a weak group. In those moments, the analyst has to evaluate whether the price is moving because the business has changed or because capital is rotating through the sector. The answer is often different from what the chart alone suggests.

Stress periods reveal these biases most clearly. When credit tightens, demand slows, or input costs jump, investors tend to search for simple explanations and quick classifications. Strong balance sheets are suddenly treated as proof of safety in every case, while leverage is treated as fatal in every case, even though the impact depends on the industry's cash conversion, refinancing needs, and pricing flexibility. Research on distress prediction has shown that early warning signals often live in financial ratios and operating patterns long before failure becomes obvious [116]. The analytical task is not to predict distress perfectly, but to notice when a sector's normal assumptions about margins, funding, or demand are no longer reliable.

One of the best ways to reduce these traps is to force the analysis to move from story to structure. Instead of asking whether the company "looks good," ask what part of the industry's economics supports that view. Instead of asking whether the sector is "cheap," ask whether the current multiple reflects a temporary dislocation, a cyclical trough, or a permanent change in profitability. Instead of asking whether management sounds confident, ask whether the peer set is showing the same pattern in orders, pricing, inventories, or capital spending. Sector analysis becomes more accurate when it is treated as a test of assumptions rather than a search for reassurance.

Citations

The following sources were referenced in the preceding chapters. Each entry links back to the inline reference in the text. All sources were verified against the OpenAlex academic database at the time of generation.

1. J. W. Kijne, Randolph Barker, David Molden (2004). Water productivity in agriculture: limits and opportunities for improvement. https://doi.org/10.5860/choice.42-0937

2. Michael D. Clemes, Christopher Gan, Dongmei Zhang (2010). Customer switching behaviour in the Chinese retail banking industry. https://doi.org/10.1108/02652321011085185

3. John G. Meara, Andrew Leather, Lars Hagander et al. (2015). Global Surgery 2030: evidence and solutions for achieving health, welfare, and economic development. https://doi.org/10.1016/s0140-6736(15)60160-x

4. Thomas W. Hertel, Hertel, Thomas W. (1999). Applied General Equilibrium Analysis of Agricultural and Resource Policies. https://doi.org/10.22004/ag.econ.283436

5. Arild Angelsen, Sven Wunder (2003). Exploring the forest--poverty link: key concepts, issues and research implications. https://doi.org/10.17528/cifor/001211

6. Ming-Lang Tseng, Tat-Dat Bui, Ming K. Lim et al. (2021). Comparing world regional sustainable supply chain finance using big data analytics: a bibliometric analysis. https://doi.org/10.1108/imds-09-2020-0521

7. Thomas W. Hertel (2000). Applied General Equilibrium Analysis of Agricultural and Resource Policies. https://doi.org/10.21642/gtap.wp03

8. Mario Situm (2023). Financial distress in the Austrian tourism industry: hotels and restaurants analysis. https://doi.org/10.54055/ejtr.v34i.2992

9. Timothy C. Durham, Tamás Mizik (2021). Comparative Economics of Conventional, Organic, and Alternative Agricultural Production Systems. https://doi.org/10.3390/economies9020064

10. Thaddaeus Obaji Ariom, Elodie Dimon, Eva Nambeye et al. (2022). Climate-Smart Agriculture in African Countries: A Review of Strategies and Impacts on Smallholder Farmers. https://doi.org/10.3390/su141811370

11. Ramon George Atento (2025). Valuation Metrics, Market Efficiency, and Investor Sentiment: A Descriptive Analysis of Philippine Stock Exchange–Listed Firms. https://doi.org/10.65166/6kbeat87

12. S. P. Deighton, R. C. Dix, J. Ross Graham et al. (2009). Governance and Risk Management in United Kingdom Insurance Companies. https://doi.org/10.1017/s1357321700005729

13. Friedrich Sayn-Wittgenstein, Frédéric de Mariz, Christina Leijonhufvud (2025). Nature Finance: Bridging Natural and Financial Capital Through Robust Impact Measurement. https://doi.org/10.3390/risks13110213

14. OECD (2020). ESG Investing. https://doi.org/10.1787/5504598c-en

15. Li-Chin Jennifer Ho, Qunfeng Liao, Martin E. Taylor (2015). Real and Accrual-Based Earnings Management in the Pre- and Post-IFRS Periods: Evidence from China. https://doi.org/10.1111/jifm.12030

16. Helena Isidro, Dhananjay Nanda, Peter D. Wysocki (2019). On the Relation between Financial Reporting Quality and Country Attributes: Research Challenges and Opportunities. https://doi.org/10.2308/accr-52607

17. Mark H. Lang, Lorien Stice-Lawrence (2021). Textual analysis and international financial reporting: Large sample evidence. https://doi.org/10.17615/k1q1-fp59

18. Cécile Carpentier, Douglas J. Cumming, Jean-Marc Suret (2010). The Valuation Effect of Listing Requirements: An Analysis of Venture Capital-Backed IPOs. https://openalex.org/W2125647111

19. Ray Ball (2009). Market and Political/Regulatory Perspectives on the Recent Accounting Scandals. https://doi.org/10.1111/j.1475-679x.2009.00325.x

20. IPBES (2019). Summary for policymakers of the global assessment report on biodiversity and ecosystem services. https://doi.org/10.5281/zenodo.3553579

21. Nathalie Seddon, Alison Smith, Pete Smith et al. (2021). Getting the message right on nature-based solutions to climate change. https://doi.org/10.1111/gcb.15513

22. Marinda Weideman (2006). Land reform, equity and growth in South Africa: A comparative analysis. https://openalex.org/W2234853912

23. Jacob A. Bikker, Barbara Casu, Claudia Girardone et al. (2009). Productivity in the Financial Services Sector. https://openalex.org/W182215571

24. Aigul P. Salina (2017). Financial soundness of Kazakhstan banks : analysis and prediction. https://openalex.org/W2892350601

25. Carolina Castaldi (2018). To trademark or not to trademark: The case of the creative and cultural industries. https://doi.org/10.1016/j.respol.2018.01.006

26. Maria Korban, Mari Westby Nordstrøm (2015). The brand management system (BMS) : its facilitators, impediments, and consequences. https://openalex.org/W2495369004

27. Athanasios (2010). The Importance of Information through Accounting Practice in Agricultural Sector-European Data Network. https://doi.org/10.3844/jssp.2010.221.228

28. Laura Restrepo Campuzano, Gustavo Adolfo Hincapié Llanos, Jhon Wilder Zartha Sossa et al. (2023). Barriers to the Adoption of Innovations for Sustainable Development in the Agricultural Sector—Systematic Literature Review (SLR). https://doi.org/10.3390/su15054374

29. Lennart Ante (2020). A place next to Satoshi: foundations of blockchain and cryptocurrency research in business and economics. https://doi.org/10.1007/s11192-020-03492-8

30. Michael J. Roth, Steven G. Smith (1995). Land tenure, land markets, and institutional transformation in Zambia. https://openalex.org/W1564030492

31. OECD (2025). Mapping Ukraine's Financial Markets and Corporate Governance Framework for a Sustainable Recovery. https://doi.org/10.1787/866c5c44-en

32. Licínio C. Lima, Paula Guimarães (2011). European Strategies in Lifelong Learning: A Critical Introduction. https://doi.org/10.3224/86649444

33. O.V. Narimanova (2024). RUSSIAN PHARMACY IN THE CONTEXT OF THE CORONAVIRUS PANDEMIC. https://doi.org/10.34660/inf.2021.42.28.003

34. Vyacheslav Afanasyev (2010). Evaluating Ukraine's agro-industrial sector: comprehensive assessment with the view of sustainability improvement and European integration. https://openalex.org/W3158598311

35. Yochanan Altman, Judi Neal, Wolfgang Mayrhofer (2022). Workplace Spirituality. https://doi.org/10.1515/9783110711349

36. Lourdes Casanova, Andrea Golstein, André Abreu de Almeida et al. (2009). From Multilatinas to Global Latinas: The New Latin

American Multinationals (Compilation Case Studies). https://doi.org/10.18235/0012383

37. Oludolapo Makinde (2019). Developing corporate governance in Nigeria : lessons from a comparative analysis of Nigerian and Canadian corporate governance frameworks. https://doi.org/10.14288/1.0380537

38. Patrick Honohan, Donal Donovan, Paul K. Gorecki et al. (2010). The Irish Banking Crisis: Regulatory and Financial Stability Policy. https://openalex.org/W2121781357

39. Dani Menachem Yudelowitz (2008). The interpretation of market related information and data in the South African residential property market affects at what stage each individual party lies in the real estate market. https://openalex.org/W2237855494

40. Universidad Politécnica de Tlaxcala, César Saldaña-Carro, Román Torres-Romero et al. (2024). Finance and Business: Economic Challenges and Expectations. https://doi.org/10.35429/h.2024.13.1.126

41. Klaus Abbink, A Abbink, Klaus Kuon et al. (2000). Abstracts of Working Papers in Economics. https://doi.org/10.1017/s0951007900004915

42. Feng Ma, Jiawei Cao, Yizhi Wang et al. (2023). Dissecting climate change risk and financial market instability: Implications for ecological risk management. https://doi.org/10.1111/risa.14265

43. Eleftherios Thalassinos, Konstantinos Liapis, John E. Thalassinos (2011). "The Regulation Framework for the Banking Sector: The EMU, European Banks and Rating Agencies before and during the Recent Financial and Debt Crisis". https://openalex.org/W1963546739

44. Laurence J. Kotlikoff (1984). Taxation and Savings - A Neoclassical Perspective. https://doi.org/10.3386/w1302

45. Unknown author (2023). India's Financial System. https://doi.org/10.5089/9798400223525.071

46. Olasunbo Olajumoke Fagbore, Jeffrey Chidera Ogeawuchi, Oluwatosin Ilori et al. (2023). Financial Statement Analysis Models for Strategic Insights in Private Wealth and Capital Markets. https://doi.org/10.62225/2583049x.2023.3.6.4332

47. Panisa Mechinda, Sirivan Serirat, Nongluck Popaijit et al. (2010). The Relative Impact Of Competitiveness Factors And Destination Equity On Tourists Loyalty In Koh Chang, Thailand. https://doi.org/10.19030/iber.v9i10.643

48. Kerri L. Steenwerth, Amanda K. Hodson, Arnold J. Bloom et al. (2014). Climate-smart agriculture global research agenda: scientific basis for action. https://doi.org/10.1186/2048-7010-3-11

49. World Bank (2019). Ethiopia Financial Sector Development. https://doi.org/10.1596/34065

50. Gregory S. Crawford, Nicola Pavanini, Fabiano Schivardi (2018). Asymmetric Information and Imperfect Competition in Lending Markets. https://doi.org/10.1257/aer.20150487

51. Barbara Grabińska, Marcin Kędzior, Dorota Kędzior et al. (2021). The Impact of Corporate Governance on the Capital Structure of Companies from the Energy Industry. The Case of Poland. https://doi.org/10.3390/en14217412

52. Douglas W. Diamond, Yunzhi Hu, Raghuram G. Rajan (2017). Pledgeability, Industry Liquidity, and Financing Cycles. https://doi.org/10.3386/w23055

53. Mark Bunting (2020). Dimensions and indicators of non-profit financial condition: Evidence from South African public universities. https://doi.org/10.4102/sajems.v23i1.2974

54. Avner Offer (2003). Why Has the Public Sector Grown So Large in Market Societies?: The Political Economy of Prudence in the UK, C. 1870-2000. https://openalex.org/W2138021720

55. May Hald (2009). Sustainable Urban Development and the Chinese Eco-City : Concepts, Strategies, Policies and Assessments. https://openalex.org/W2466218486

56. Karel Lannoo (2015). The Great Financial Plumbing: From Northern Rock to Banking Union. CEPS Paperback, 19 October 2015. https://openalex.org/W1750171609

57. Dafydd Mali, Hyoung-Joo Lim (2023). Do rating agencies impound workforce human capital information into default risk assessments?. https://doi.org/10.1080/01559982.2023.2235873

58. Kyle Jurado, Sydney C. Ludvigson, Serena Ng (2013). Measuring Uncertainty. https://doi.org/10.3386/w19456

59. Peter Conti-Brown, Yair Listokin, Nicholas R. Parrillo (2021). Towards an Administrative Law of Central Banking. https://openalex.org/W3127263224

60. Christophe Faugère (2024). Velocity of Money and Productivity Growth: Explaining the 2% Inflation Target in the U.S. (1959–2007). https://doi.org/10.3390/ijfs12010015

61. Andrew Pd, A Acemoglu, Daron Angrist et al. (2000). Abstracts of Working Papers in Economics. https://doi.org/10.1017/s0951007900005039

62. Jared Steven Berenter (2013). Expanding the Central Bank mandate in the "Soy Republic" : an assessment of the impact of Central Bank governance on agricultural competitiveness and interest articulation in Argentina. https://openalex.org/W2125901542

63. Oleg Bondarenko, Carole Bernard (2020). Option-Implied Dependence and Correlation Risk Premium. https://doi.org/10.2139/ssrn.3618705

64. Lea-Marija Bevanda, Azra Zaimović, Almira Arnaut-Berilo (2021). Performance of Value and Growth Stocks in the Aftermath of the Global Financial Crisis. https://doi.org/10.2478/bsrj-2021-0032

65. Iris H-Y Chiu, Andreas Kokkinis, Andrea Miglionico (2021). Relief and rescue: financial regulatory suspensions in the United Kingdom. https://openalex.org/W3174422796

66. Armenia Androniceanu, Irina Virginia Dragulanescu (2017). Loan Policies and Economic Development in a Globalized Environment. https://doi.org/10.22364/ncebd.ab.2017.01

67. Yudhvir Seetharam (2012). Fusion investing: an esoteric approach to portfolio formation. https://openalex.org/W2121136745

68. Bryan Kelly, Dacheng Xiu (2023). Financial Machine Learning. https://doi.org/10.3386/w31502

69. Sureyya Burcu Avci, Cindy A. Schipani, H. Nejat Seyhun (2018). Do Independent Directors Curb Financial Fraud? The Evidence and Proposals for Further Reform. https://openalex.org/W2610108795

70. Xun Lei (2018). Empirical Analysis of the Link between Politics and Stock Market Behaviour. https://openalex.org/W2810730968

71. Roberto R. Rocha, Zsofia Arvai, Subika Farazi (2011). Financial Access and Stability. https://doi.org/10.1596/978-0-8213-8835-8

72. Purwanto Purwanto, Chelsea Risa Bina (2016). Analysis of Financial Ratio towards Earning Growth in Mining Companies. https://doi.org/10.13189/ujibm.2016.040301

73. Raonic, I., Isidro, H. (2012). Firm Incentives, Institutional Complexity and the Quality of "Harmonized" Accounting Numbers. https://doi.org/10.1016/j.intacc.2012.10.007

74. Antônio Lopo Martinez (2013). Earnings management in Brazil: a survey of the literature. https://doi.org/10.15728/bbr.2013.10.4.1

75. Dieter Helm (2009). Infrastructure investment, the cost of capital, and regulation: an assessment. https://doi.org/10.1093/oxrep/grp027

76. Mika Vaihekoski, Habeeb Yahya (2025). Environmental, Social, and Governance (ESG) and Firm Valuation: The Moderating Role of Audit Quality. https://doi.org/10.3390/jrfm18030148

77. Adrian D. Uzea (2009). Canadian consumer valuation of farm animal welfare and quality verification – the case of pork. https://openalex.org/W1489368231

78. Alan Batista, Miguel Calmon, Suzanna Lund et al. (2021). Investing in Native Tree Species and Agroforestry Systems in Brazil: An Economic Valuation. https://doi.org/10.46830/wrirpt.18.00066en

79. Petra Hellegers, Christopher J. Perry, Hellegers, Petra J.G.J. et al. (2004). WATER AS AN ECONOMIC GOOD IN IRRIGATED AGRICULTURE: THEORY AND PRACTICE. https://doi.org/10.22004/ag.econ.29109

80. Abigail Bugbee Brown (2007). Private Firms Working in the Public Interest: Is the Financial Statement Audit Broken?. https://doi.org/10.7249/rgsd212

81. Rosella Carè, Rabia Fatima (2024). Financial Market Misconduct: A Bibliometric Perspective. https://doi.org/10.1111/eufm.12525

82. Poh Seng Yeoh (2007). The Legal Implications of Off Balance Sheet Financing: A Comparative Analysis of UK and US Positions. https://doi.org/10.1007/978-94-024-1079-2_36

83. Thierry Bracke, Matthieu Bussière, Michael Fidora et al. (2008). A Framework for Assessing Global Imbalances. https://doi.org/10.2139/ssrn.1005942

84. Paul Guthiga (2007). Economic Assessment of Different Management Approaches of Kakamega Forest in Kenya: Cost-benefit and Local Community Satisfaction Analysis. https://openalex.org/W2261096641

85. Indra Abeysekera (2021). Intellectual Capital and Knowledge Management Research towards Value Creation. From the Past to the Future. https://doi.org/10.3390/jrfm14060238

86. Michael Adelowotan (2014). Human capital disclosure in corporate annual reports. https://openalex.org/W2117342695

87. Athula S Manawaduge (2012). Corporate governance practices and their impacts on corporate performance in an emerging market: the case of Sri Lanka. https://openalex.org/W65908410

88. R. Paul Bardos, Hayley Thomas, Jonathan W. N. Smith et al. (2020). Sustainability assessment framework and indicators developed by SuRF-UK for land remediation option appraisal. https://doi.org/10.1002/rem.21668

89. M. Sohail, Sue Cavill (2007). Partnering to Combat Corruption in Infrastructure Services: A Toolkit. https://openalex.org/W1211779415

90. Byungguk Ko, Kyu-Hwan Lee, Yong-Beum Yoon et al. (2022). Impact of ESG (Environmental, Social, Governance) on the Performance of Electric Utilities. https://doi.org/10.7849/ksnre.2022.0010

91. Adam D. Dixon, PATRICK J. SCHENA, Javier Capapé (2022). Sovereign Wealth Funds. https://doi.org/10.2307/j.ctv2tjdhjj

92. Alejandro Acevedo Amorocho, José Gerardo De la Vega Meneses, Ángel Acevedo-Duque et al. (2026). Construction and Validation of a 5P–ESG Composite Index for Sustainable Corporate Governance and Financial Analysis in Emerging Markets: Evidence from the MSCI COLCAP. https://doi.org/10.20944/preprints202602.0752.v1

93. Lizelle Engelbrecht (2015). The role of hedonic and utilitarian shopping motivations in males' fashion leadership behaviour in Gauteng. https://openalex.org/W2479253095

94. Roberto Graña-Álvarez, Jacobo Gomez-Conde, Ernesto Lopez-Valeiras et al. (2024). Management control systems, business financial

literacy and financial leverage in business-incubated start-ups. https://doi.org/10.1016/j.bar.2024.101427

95. Emil Holmberg, Hans Jeppsson (2011). The use of valuation models by European biotechnology analysts. https://openalex.org/W1954978741

96. Vilma Karvonen (2010). Marketing investment courage and financial performance- A study of profiles and financial implications among Finnish firms. https://openalex.org/W2597789247

97. Michael Colin Glensor (2010). Organisational change management in South Africa : the development of a change framework and scorecard within a mergers and aquisitions environment. https://openalex.org/W1537885992

98. Evan Mills, Jessica Granderson, Rengie Chan et al. (2015). Green, Clean, & Mean: Pushing the Energy Envelope in Tech Industry Buildings. https://doi.org/10.2172/1342751

99. Thi Phi, ティ フィ (2017). A comprehensive study of accounting system and consolidated accounting in vietnam:focusing on the factor analysis of consolidated financial statements. https://doi.org/10.69200/0002000258

100. Kenton K. Yee (2007). A Bayesian Framework for Combining Valuation Estimates. https://doi.org/10.48550/arxiv.0707.3482

101. José Luís Miralles Quirós, María del Mar Miralles Quirós, José Manuel Nogueira (2020). Sustainable Development Goals and Investment Strategies: The Profitability of Using Five-Factor Fama-French Alphas. https://doi.org/10.3390/su12051842

102. Lonwabo Mlawu, Frank Ranganai Matenda, Mabutho Sibanda (2025). Incentives for Accrual-Based Earnings Management in Emerging Economies—A Systematic Literature Review with Bibliometric Analysis. https://doi.org/10.3390/admsci15060209

103. Laurence B. Siegel, Barclay Douglas, Clifford Asness et al. (2003). Benchmarks and Investment Management. https://doi.org/10.2470/rf.v2003.n1.3922

104. Waldemar Tarczyński, Małgorzata Łuniewska (2017). Application of The Leading Sector Identification Method in The Portfolio Analysis. https://doi.org/10.18778/0208-6018.328.12

105. Diandian Ma (2014). Momentum, Acceleration and Non-Linearities in Equity Valuation on the Shanghai Stock Exchange. https://doi.org/10.26686/wgtn.17006440

106. Paul Gouvard, Amir Goldberg, Sameer B. Srivastava (2023). Doing Organizational Identity: Earnings Surprises and the Performative Atypicality Premium. https://doi.org/10.31235/osf.io/3fyb9

107. Benjamin Austin, Edward Glaeser, Lawrence H. Summers (2018). Jobs for the Heartland: Place-Based Policies in 21st-Century America. https://doi.org/10.1353/eca.2018.0002

108. R. Seppaelae, Clark Row, A. Morgan (1983). Forest Sector Models. https://openalex.org/W2759698622

109. Luigi Buttiglione, Philip R. Lane, Lucrezia Reichlin et al. (2016). Deleveraging? What Deleveraging?. https://openalex.org/W3011816170

110. International Monetary Fund. Western Hemisphere Dept. (2021). United States: 2021 Article IV Consultation-Press Release; Staff Report; and Statement by the Executive Director for the United States. https://doi.org/10.5089/9781513591810.002

111. Maksym Bezpartochnyi (2020). Strategies for sustainable socio-economic development and mechanisms their implementation in the global dimension. https://doi.org/10.6084/m9.figshare.11839209

112. O. V. Buklemishev, Yu. A. Danilov (2018). INTERNATIONALIZATION OF RUBLE: MYTHS AND ECONOMIC POLICY. https://doi.org/10.20542/0131-2227-2018-62-12-26-34

113. Sarah Jacobson (2023). Careers in cross-cultural context : women bank managers in Finland and in the United States.. https://doi.org/10.7275/20483264

114. Daniel J.H. Greenwood (2019). Enronitis: Why Good Corporations Go Bad. https://doi.org/10.7916/abky-cf70

115. Jayampathy I. Samarakoon, Maeve Nightingale, Hermes, Rudi et al. (2021). Review of community-based ICM: best practices and lessons learned in the Bay of Bengal, South Asia. https://openalex.org/W2295024648

116. Mohamed Ouadani (2026). Study for the bankruptcy prediction using machine learning: modeling bankruptcy risk of companies based on financial ratios, using supervised learning to support credit and investment decisions. https://openalex.org/W7134152927

117. Rebecca Pearce (2013). Blind belief in a commodified natural resource : a grounded theory. https://openalex.org/W778866533

118. Muhammad Shaukat Malik (2017). Financial statement analysis, internal controls, and audit readiness: Bestpractices for Pakistan army financial management officers. https://openalex.org/W2900330169

119. Jamie Donovan (2015). A framework for evaluating automated valuation models in real estate: an auditing perspective. https://openalex.org/W2581217281

120. Donovan, Jamie (2015). Automaattiset arvonmääritysmallit kiinteistöalalla: auditoinnin näkökulma. https://openalex.org/W7113156130

121. Heniwati, Elok, Heniwati, Elok (n.d.). Post-IFRS Outcome on Financial Reporting Information : Early Evidence from Indonesian Stock Exchange. https://openalex.org/W7052120316

122. International Monetary Fund (2010). Bangladesh: Financial System Stability Assessment. https://doi.org/10.5089/9781451804287.002

123. Kesseven Padachi, H. R. Urdhin, Mootooganagen Ramen (2016). Assessing Corporate Governance Practices of Mauritian Companies. https://doi.org/10.5296/ijafr.v6i1.9281

124. Giorgos Somarakis, Stagakis, Stavros, Chrysoulakis, Nektarios (2019). ThinkNature / Nature-Based Solutions Handbook. https://doi.org/10.26225/jerv-w202

125. Erick Meira de Oliveira (2015). CORPORATE SOCIAL RESPONSIBILITY AND FIRM PERFORMANCE: A CASE STUDY FROM THE BRAZILIAN ELECTRIC SECTOR. https://doi.org/10.17771/pucrio.acad.25647

126. José Manuel Santos Jaén, Gema Martín de Almagro-Vázquez, María del Carmen Valls Martínez (2023). Is earnings management impacted by audit fees and auditor tenure? An analysis of the Big Four audit firms in the US market. https://doi.org/10.24136/oc.2023.027

127. Geert Braam, Ferdy van Beest (2013). A Conceptually-Based Empirical Analysis on Quality Differences between UK Annual Reports and US 10-K Reports. https://openalex.org/W1485139607

128. International Monetary Fund (2014). Switzerland: Report on Observance of Standards and Codes. https://doi.org/10.5089/9781498334969.002

129. Guido Max Mantovani, Alexander Kostyuk, Dmytro Govorun (2022). Corporate governance: Next stop?. https://doi.org/10.22495/cgtaped

Conclusion

The most useful sector and industry analysis is not the kind that produces a single dramatic forecast. It is the kind that steadily improves judgment. Over time, it teaches the analyst where earnings are likely to be durable, where margins are vulnerable, where valuation is being stretched by optimism, and where the market may be misreading a temporary condition as a permanent one. That discipline matters because financial terrain is uneven. A business can be excellent and still be a poor investment if it is operating in a weakening industry structure or at the wrong point in its cycle. A business can also look ordinary on a company-only basis and still offer strong opportunity if its sector is entering a favorable phase and its peer group is being repriced for better conditions.

This is why sector and industry analysis should be treated as a framework for interpretation rather than a separate category of opinion. It helps the investor ask better questions before capital is committed. Is the company's growth being driven by broad demand, by pricing power, or by a temporary surge in volume? Are margins improving because the industry is becoming more efficient, or because competitors are under stress and have not yet responded? Does the valuation reflect a durable advantage, or is it simply echoing the market's current enthusiasm for the group? Those questions do not eliminate uncertainty, but they reduce the chance of drawing conclusions from incomplete context.

The method also improves comparison. Investors often search for the "best" company without first defining the field in which best should be measured. Yet a strong company is not always a strong stock, and a cheap stock is not always a bargain. The difference depends on the structure of the industry, the phase of the cycle, and the expectations already embedded in price. Sector analysis makes those comparisons more disciplined. It clarifies whether a company is leading or merely benefiting from a favorable backdrop, whether its returns are likely to persist, and whether its financial results are being amplified or distorted by conditions shared across the group.

For earnings analysis, this perspective is especially important. Reported results often contain signals that are easy to miss when the focus stays on the headline number alone. A revenue beat may reflect industry-wide demand that lifted several firms at once. A margin miss may reflect cost pressure that is affecting an entire peer set. A guidance change may be less about management confidence than about changes in inventory, credit, regulation, or customer behavior. In industries where customer relationships are sticky and switching is costly, earnings may be more stable than the market expects; in industries with intense competition and low retention, even a modest change in behavior can quickly alter the outlook [2].

The same logic applies to the language companies use to describe themselves. Annual reports, earnings releases, and management commentary are not just disclosures; they are evidence of how firms present their own economics. Research on financial reporting text shows that disclosure length, boilerplate language, and complexity can vary systematically with regulation and incentives [17]. That does not mean every long report is evasive or every concise report is transparent. It does mean the analyst should treat narrative as part of the sector picture, not as a substitute for it. In some industries, the wording itself may reveal how much explanation is needed to defend a weak trend, a changing model, or a less comparable set of results.

There is also a broader lesson that extends beyond any one industry: sector analysis works best when it respects the interaction between the company and its environment. A firm is not simply a self-contained earnings machine. It is embedded in a system of customers, suppliers, competitors, regulators, financing conditions, and resource constraints. In resource-based industries, for example, output and profitability can depend heavily on the efficient use of scarce inputs, and the limits of those inputs shape what is economically possible [1]. The analyst who understands that interaction can distinguish between a company that is genuinely improving and one that is merely riding a favorable external tide.

That is the deeper value of the framework. It helps investors move from isolated observation to structured interpretation. It supports better screening, better valuation, better timing, and better risk control, but only because it forces each of those tasks to be read in context. The goal is not to predict every move in advance. The goal is to recognize which forces are likely to matter most, which signals are likely to mislead, and which comparisons are actually meaningful. Once that habit is in place, sector and industry analysis becomes less of a specialty tool and more of a basic requirement for serious fundamental work.

Used that way, it strengthens nearly every part of the investment process. It sharpens the reading of earnings quality. It improves the odds of identifying businesses whose advantages are structural rather than temporary. It makes valuation more realistic by anchoring it to the economics of the field. And it gives the investor a clearer sense of when to be patient, when to be selective, and when to step aside. The market will always reward certainty more than it deserves. Sector and industry analysis helps replace that certainty with something more useful: informed judgment under real-world conditions.

Appendix: Tools, Templates, and Reference Checklists

The material that follows is designed to make the framework usable, not merely understandable. Once the sector, industry, and earnings context has been established, the next step is to carry that judgment into a form that can be repeated, compared, and revisited without starting from scratch each time. The tools in this appendix are intentionally compact: they are meant to help organize research, standardize comparisons, and keep attention on the factors that matter most when a business is being judged within its own economic setting. In practice, disciplined templates and checklists serve the same purpose as a good audit trail in financial reporting—they improve consistency, reduce omission risk, and make assumptions easier to review later [118]. The goal here is not to replace analysis, but to give it a structure that can be applied across sectors, industries, and market conditions with greater confidence.

Sector analysis checklist

A useful sector analysis checklist is less about collecting more data and more about forcing the right sequence of questions. The first pass should confirm that the company is being judged in the correct economic neighborhood: sector, industry, and subindustry. If that classification is loose or misleading, every later comparison becomes less reliable. The same is true of the business model itself. Before looking at valuation or momentum, ask whether the company earns money through recurring subscriptions, project work, transaction fees, commodity exposure, regulated pricing, or some combination of these. That answer determines which financial measures deserve the most attention and which peer group is actually relevant.

Once the business is placed correctly, the next step is to identify the sector forces that can move the whole group at once. The checklist should ask what macro variables matter most here: growth, rates, inflation, credit, labor, input costs, and currency. Not every variable matters equally, and not every industry reacts in the same direction. A capital-intensive business may be highly rate-sensitive, while a consumer-facing business may be more exposed to wage pressure or discretionary spending trends. The point of the checklist is not to produce a macro forecast; it is to connect the macro environment to the earnings drivers that matter for this specific industry.

The third layer is industry structure. A company can post good results inside an industry that is becoming more crowded, more price competitive, or more exposed to substitution. The checklist should therefore ask whether the industry has durable barriers to entry, meaningful scale advantages, strong switching costs, network effects, or regulatory protection. It should also ask whether rivalry is intensifying, whether customers are gaining bargaining power, and whether new capacity is likely to pressure margins. These questions matter because industry structure often sets the range of possible outcomes before management execution enters the picture. In infrastructure and other service-heavy sectors, corruption and governance weaknesses can also distort the apparent economics of an industry, making the quality of the operating environment itself part of the analysis [89].

After structure comes performance. The checklist should compare the company's growth, margins, and cash generation against true peers, not just the broad market. Revenue growth should be separated into volume, price, mix, acquisition effects, and recovery from prior weakness. Margins should be read in context: are they expanding because the company has genuine pricing power, or because input costs have temporarily eased? Cash flow should be checked against reported earnings to see whether profits are being converted into actual liquidity. A recurring gap between earnings and cash often tells a more important story than the headline income statement does.

Balance sheet strength belongs on the same page as the income statement, because sector economics often determine how much leverage is normal and how much is dangerous. The checklist should ask whether the industry requires heavy fixed assets, large inventories, long project cycles, or constant refinancing. It should also ask whether debt is funding growth, supporting operations, or masking weak cash generation. In some sectors, leverage is part of the model; in others, it is a warning sign. The right question is not whether debt exists, but whether the company can service it comfortably across a full cycle and still invest enough to remain competitive.

Valuation should be the last major block, not the first. The checklist should compare the company's multiple with its own history, its direct peers, and the industry's normal range for growth, risk, and capital intensity. A stock may appear expensive on an absolute basis while still being reasonable for a business with superior returns on capital and durable demand. The reverse is also true: a low multiple can hide weak economics, poor reinvestment opportunities, or a structurally challenged industry. Relative valuation works best when it is anchored to the same sector context that shaped the operating results in the first place.

Finally, the checklist should end with a judgment about durability. Ask what would have to remain true for the current thesis to work: stable pricing, continued demand, favorable regulation, manageable input costs, or disciplined competition. Then ask what would break it: slower end-market growth, margin compression, funding stress, or a shift in customer behavior. Research on human capital disclosure in annual reports shows that firms in information- and technology-driven environments increasingly rely on intangible capabilities as value drivers [86], which is a reminder that some of the most important sector variables are not always visible in the headline numbers. A good checklist does not eliminate uncertainty, but it makes uncertainty explicit, which is the difference between a repeatable process and a one-time opinion.

Industry comparison template

A useful industry comparison starts by forcing the analyst to compare like with like. The purpose is not to produce a beautiful spreadsheet; it is to make sure that the numbers being compared actually reflect similar economics. Two companies can share the same broad sector label and still differ materially in customer concentration, revenue recognition, capital intensity, margin structure, and balance sheet risk. A comparison template keeps those differences visible instead of letting them disappear inside a single valuation multiple or growth rate.

The first line of the template should identify the company's exact placement in the market map. That means sector, industry, and sub-industry, plus a brief note on the business model. The business model note matters because labels are often too broad to be useful on their own. A software company may sell recurring subscriptions, usage-based services, or one-time licenses. A bank may be a consumer lender, a commercial lender, a custodian, or a payments intermediary. A retailer may be a price leader, a premium brand, or a high-turnover distributor. Each model creates different earnings patterns, and the comparison should reflect that before any financial ratios are reviewed.

After classification, the template should define the peer set. This is where many comparisons go wrong. The right peer group is usually not the largest companies in the sector or the most familiar names in the market. It is the set of firms with similar economics, similar customer behavior, and similar constraints on growth and profitability. A template should record why each peer was selected and whether any were excluded because of a different revenue mix, geographic exposure, regulatory regime, or capital structure. If the peer set is not deliberate, the analysis becomes a comparison of convenience rather than a comparison of substance.

Once the peer set is fixed, the next step is to capture the core operating drivers that explain performance. A practical template usually includes revenue growth, gross margin, operating margin, return on invested capital, free cash flow margin, leverage, and liquidity. Those metrics should be viewed alongside the variables that make them meaningful in the industry: average selling price, volume growth, customer retention, churn, backlog, utilization, same-store sales, loan growth, reserve coverage, or capacity additions, depending on the business. The point is to connect the reported results to the operating engine underneath them. A margin that looks strong may simply reflect a favorable mix shift; a growth rate that looks ordinary may hide unusually efficient capital use.

It also helps to separate structural measures from cyclical measures. Structural measures describe the long-run economics of the industry, such as pricing power, switching costs, asset intensity, regulatory burden, and competitive concentration. Cyclical measures describe the current phase of demand, inventory, credit, or cost pressure. A company may look cheap because earnings are temporarily depressed, but the template should show whether that weakness is cyclical or structural. That distinction matters because a low multiple is more attractive when the industry is temporarily out of favor than when the business model itself is under permanent pressure. In sectors where external factors such as audit quality, governance, or disclosure practices can affect how valuation is interpreted, those items should be noted as well; recent research finds that ESG scores can be associated with higher valuation when audit quality is stronger [76].

The template should then compare valuation in context, not in isolation. A simple list of price-to-earnings or enterprise-value-to-EBITDA multiples is not enough. The analyst should record whether the company trades at a premium or discount to its peer median, how wide that spread is, and whether the spread is justified by growth, margin quality, balance sheet strength, or return on capital. If the company is expensive, the template should ask what the market is paying for. If it is cheap, the template should ask what risk the market is discounting. This avoids the common mistake of treating every discount as an opportunity and every premium as a warning. Some businesses deserve persistent premiums because their economics are more durable; others deserve discounts because their earnings are more fragile.

A disciplined comparison template should also include a short qualitative field for industry-specific risks and catalysts. This is where the analyst records items that do not fit neatly into a ratio but still shape the investment case: pricing pressure, regulation, product cycles, commodity exposure, labor sensitivity, litigation risk, customer concentration, technology disruption, or capital spending requirements. The same field can note near-term catalysts such as inventory normalization, new capacity, contract renewals, rate changes, or policy shifts. These notes keep the comparison from becoming static. Industries are not fixed objects; they move through phases, and the template should preserve the reason a company may be leading or lagging at the moment of review.

A simple working format is often enough if it is used consistently. For each company, the analyst can record the following: classification, peer group, business model, key operating drivers, recent financial trends, valuation versus peers, balance sheet profile, industry risks, and the current judgment on quality and attractiveness. The value of the template is not in its complexity but in its repeatability. When the same structure is applied across companies, the analyst can see whether differences in valuation are supported by differences in economics, or whether the market is pricing one business as if it belonged to a stronger industry than it really does. That is the real function of comparison: to make hidden assumptions visible before capital is committed.

Earnings quality review guide

Earnings quality review begins with a simple question: how much of the reported profit reflects durable economics, and how much reflects timing, judgment, or transitory conditions? In sector and industry analysis, that question cannot be answered by looking at net income alone. A company can report rising earnings while its underlying business is weakening, just as it can report flat or declining earnings while building a stronger long-term position. The review therefore starts by separating the recurring from the incidental. Revenue growth should be checked for dependence on one-time price increases, channel loading, unusually easy comparisons, or temporary demand spikes. Margin expansion should be tested for operating leverage that can persist versus cost cuts that cannot. If the earnings story depends too heavily on events that are unlikely to repeat, the quality of those earnings is lower than the headline number suggests.

The first layer of review is the relationship between revenue recognition and business reality. In many industries, reported growth can outpace true demand because of billing timing, extended payment terms, inventory movements, or aggressive recognition practices. This is especially important in sectors where contracts, installations, projects, or financial estimates play a large role in the accounting. A retail chain may show strong same-period revenue because it pushed product into the channel ahead of actual sell-through. A services firm may book revenue before the cash is collected and before the customer relationship is fully proven. In both cases, the analyst should ask whether the revenue is backed by customer behavior that can be observed in order flow, retention, repeat usage, or collection patterns. Where revenue depends on management judgment, reporting quality becomes more sensitive to incentives and oversight, which is why the broader accounting environment matters as well [16].

Next comes the margin review, which is often where sector effects become easiest to see. Gross margin reveals pricing power and input-cost discipline, while operating margin shows how well the business absorbs fixed overhead. But the analyst should not stop at the percentage itself. Margin quality is stronger when expansion comes from mix improvement, product differentiation, or structural scale advantages. It is weaker when it comes from reduced marketing, deferred maintenance, underinvestment in research, or temporary cost deflation that may reverse. In industries with intense competition, a short burst of margin improvement can be a sign of cyclical relief rather than durable strength. In more concentrated or regulated industries, margins may remain high for longer, but they should still be tested against customer retention, capital needs, and the likelihood of future competitive response.

Cash flow is the next checkpoint because it reveals whether accounting profits are being converted into spendable resources. A business with high earnings but weak operating cash flow may be stretching payables, building receivables, or capitalizing costs in ways that improve the appearance of performance without improving the economics. The reverse can also happen: a company may generate strong cash in a given period because working capital temporarily unwinds, even though earnings quality is not especially strong. For this reason, cash flow should be reviewed over several periods, not just one quarter. The key is consistency. Durable earnings tend to be accompanied by stable conversion from earnings to operating cash flow over time, while lower-quality earnings often show up as volatility, repeated adjustments, or persistent gaps between accrual profit and cash generation.

Working capital trends deserve special attention because they often expose whether reported growth is real or merely accelerated through the system. Rising receivables can indicate healthy sales, but they can also indicate lenient credit terms or collection pressure. Rising inventory can mean a company is preparing for demand, but it can also mean products are not moving as expected. Falling payables may reflect stronger supplier relationships, yet they can also signal that the company is using cash faster than it generates it. In sectors where inventory cycles are central to performance, these movements can tell the analyst more than the income statement alone. A company that consistently turns inventory and collects cash faster than peers usually has a stronger earnings profile than one that needs constant balance sheet support to sustain reported growth.

Balance sheet review completes the picture because earnings quality is not just about what the company earned this period, but about what it had to risk to earn it. A heavily leveraged firm may report acceptable earnings during favorable conditions, yet those earnings have less resilience if rates rise, refinancing becomes more expensive, or demand weakens. Similarly, a company with large off-balance-sheet commitments, pension obligations, or contingent liabilities may appear healthier than it really is. Sector context matters here because the normal level of leverage differs widely across industries. Still, the analyst should ask whether debt is supporting productive capacity, funding growth at acceptable returns, or simply masking weak operating performance. Where the balance sheet is stretched, reported earnings deserve more skepticism because the margin for error is smaller.

Finally, the review should test for signs of earnings management. This does not mean assuming manipulation whenever results look strong; it means recognizing that financial reporting always involves estimates, judgments, and incentives. Large accruals, repeated special items, persistent nonrecurring charges, unusual reserve releases, and sudden changes in depreciation, capitalization, or revenue timing can all affect the appearance of earnings. Audit quality and oversight matter because they influence how reliably those judgments are made, and research has shown that reporting quality is shaped by the broader institutional environment as well as by firm-level choices [19]. In practice, the best earnings quality review does not look for one dramatic red flag. It looks for alignment: between revenue and customer behavior, between margins and competitive position, between earnings and cash, and between balance sheet risk and the demands of the industry. When those elements move together, the earnings are more likely to be dependable. When they do not, the headline number may be telling only part of the story.

Glossary of key terms and metrics

Accurate sector and industry analysis depends on using the language of the market with precision. Terms that sound interchangeable in casual conversation often carry different meanings in practice, and those differences matter when comparing companies, reading filings, or interpreting valuation. A sector is the broad economic grouping that captures a large set of businesses exposed to similar demand drivers, while an industry is a narrower competitive field inside that sector. A subindustry goes one step further and groups firms with even closer operating characteristics, such as similar products, customer types, or revenue models. The narrower the grouping, the more useful it becomes for judging whether a company is truly outperforming or simply benefiting from a broad label that hides important differences.

Peer group refers to the set of companies an analyst uses for comparison. In theory, the peer group should contain businesses with similar economics, not merely similar tickers or familiar names. A strong peer group makes it easier to see whether margins, growth, leverage, and valuation are exceptional or ordinary within the company's real competitive neighborhood. Benchmark is related but not identical: it is the standard against which performance is measured, often an index, sector ETF, or custom basket. A company can outperform its benchmark and still lag its direct peers, which is why both measures deserve attention. Relative performance describes how a stock, industry, or sector is doing compared with a chosen benchmark or comparison set, and it is often the first sign that capital is rotating toward or away from a group.

Revenue growth is the rate at which sales increase over a given period, usually measured year over year. In sector work, the key question is not only how fast revenue is growing, but why. Growth may come from higher prices, greater unit volume, acquisitions, new product launches, or a rebound from a depressed base. Those sources carry different implications for durability. Organic growth usually refers to growth generated by the underlying business rather than acquisitions or one-time events. It is often a cleaner measure of demand strength because it strips out the effect of deal-making. When analysts compare industries, they often pay close attention to whether growth is broad-based or concentrated in a few companies, because concentrated growth can signal market share shifts rather than healthy expansion across the whole field.

Gross margin is revenue minus the direct cost of goods sold, expressed as a percentage of revenue. It shows how much of each sales dollar remains after the most immediate production or service costs are paid. Operating margin goes further by subtracting operating expenses such as selling, general and administrative costs, research and development, and other overhead. A company with high gross margins but weak operating margins may have a good product but an inefficient cost structure. Operating leverage describes the degree to which incremental revenue flows through to profit. Industries with high fixed costs can show powerful margin expansion when demand rises, but they can also suffer sharp margin compression when demand softens. This is one reason analysts study margins across a peer set rather than in isolation.

Cash flow from operations is the cash generated by the core business before capital spending and financing decisions. It is a critical measure because it reveals whether reported earnings are being converted into actual cash. Free cash flow is the cash left after a company funds the capital expenditures needed to maintain or expand the business. Some industries can generate strong accounting earnings while consuming large amounts of cash, especially when working capital needs are high or capital intensity is heavy. That is why cash flow quality matters. A company whose earnings are backed by cash is generally easier to trust than one whose profits depend on aggressive accruals, delayed spending, or rising receivables. Research comparing reporting quality across annual reports and 10-K fillings also underscores that disclosure practices and presentation can vary meaningfully across reporting environments [127].

Capital intensity refers to how much investment a business must make in property, equipment, infrastructure, technology, or working capital to sustain its operations and grow. A capital-intensive industry often requires more funding before growth translates into durable returns. Return on invested capital, or ROIC, measures how efficiently a company converts the capital it employs into after-tax operating profit. High ROIC can indicate a strong business model, but it should always be read in context. A company may post an attractive ROIC during a favorable part of the cycle, only to see it fall when competition intensifies or pricing weakens. Asset turnover is another useful metric, showing how much revenue is generated for each dollar of assets employed. Together, these terms help explain whether profitability is being driven by pricing power, efficiency, leverage, or a temporary cycle.

Leverage means the use of borrowed money or fixed obligations to finance operations and growth. In some sectors, leverage is a structural feature of the business model rather than a discretionary choice. That makes the distinction between manageable leverage and dangerous leverage especially important. Debt-to-equity, debt-to-EBITDA, and interest coverage are common measures used to judge whether a company can support its obligations under normal and stressed conditions. EBITDA stands for earnings before interest, taxes, depreciation, and amortization; it is often used as a rough proxy for operating cash generation, though it should not be treated as cash itself. Guidance is management's forward-looking estimate of expected results, and in sector analysis it is often read as much for tone and industry commentary as for the specific numbers. Analysts frequently use guidance to infer whether a company is seeing broad demand strength, margin pressure, inventory correction, or pricing change.

Valuation multiple is a shorthand used to compare market price with a financial measure such as earnings, sales, book value, or cash flow. Common examples include price-to-earnings, enterprise value to EBITDA, and price-to-sales. Multiples are useful because they compress several assumptions into a single number, but they can also mislead if the underlying economics are not comparable. A high multiple may reflect strong recurring revenue, low capital needs, and stable demand; a low multiple may reflect cyclical risk, weak pricing power, or heavy reinvestment requirements. Enterprise value adds debt and subtracts cash so that the market value of the entire operating business can be compared more fairly across different capital structures. Used properly, these metrics do not replace analysis; they organize it.

Volatility measures how much a stock or industry's price tends to fluctuate over time. In sector analysis, volatility is not just a trading statistic; it often reflects the predictability of earnings, the sensitivity of the business to macro conditions, and the market's confidence in the durability of cash flows. Correlation measures how closely two securities or groups move together. High correlation within a sector can indicate shared exposure to the same economic driver, while low correlation may suggest that company-specific factors matter more than the broader group. Cycle refers to the recurring pattern of expansion, slowdown, contraction, and recovery that shapes demand, margins, and sentiment over time. These terms help the analyst distinguish between a business that is temporarily out of favor and one whose economics are inherently unstable.

www.ingramcontent.com/pod-product-compliance
Lightning Source LLC
LaVergne TN
LVHW100315210926
848480LV00003B/1135